LIVING ON *Memories*

LYNNE OAKES

ISBN: 979-8-89419-188-1 (sc)
ISBN: 979-8-89419-189-8 (hc)
ISBN: 979-8-89419-190-4 (e)

THE EWINGS PUBLISHING

One Galleria Blvd., Suite 1900, Metairie, LA 70001
(504) 702-6708

For Bob and Frances

Contents

Introduction

It began with a box. A box that had crumbled in the attic. A box that contained 180 letters and three diaries from over 70 years ago. The letters were my father's correspondence to my mother during his military service in World War II. Letters from January 1943 to October 1944. During this time, my parents, Bob and Frances, wrote to each other almost daily. Phone calls were possible during WWII, but they were difficult to carry out and expensive for a common soldier. There were no cell phones, computers, or other methods of communication. Hand-written letters were still the most common way to connect.

Bob was not the best writer, but he was prolific, sincere, and funny. He chronicled the life he experienced as an airman, the future he hoped for, and his love for Frances. Unfortunately, Frances' letters to Bob during the war were lost, as his personal belongings did not make it home with him. What did survive, however, were Frances' diaries from when they first met as teenagers.

This is the story of Bob and Frances, their experiences and their love for one another. It is also the story of two people who found themselves caught in some of the worst circumstances imaginable. Like millions of other ordinary people, they were asked to endure separation, face fears of constant uncertainty, and exhibit courage on an extraordinary scale. Their story parallels that of countless other young couples who were asked to sacrifice and serve their country during WWII.

I have had the privilege of talking with other WWII veterans. When I asked why they joined the military to serve in WWII, they simply answered that it was their duty. My father and my mother, as with other men and women of this time, straightforwardly and without questioning, fulfilled their duty, saving the world in the process.

When I was a child, my brothers and I were not allowed to inquire about Dad's war experiences. We hardly knew what a war was or that our father had served in the Army Air Force. When I was eight, I found a box containing Dad's medals from the war. When I showed them to my parents, I was scolded. This was obviously a forbidden topic, and I did not broach the subject again until I was an adult.

Years later, my son asked his grandpa to come and speak to his fifth-grade class on Veterans Day about his service in WWII. We were sure that Dad would refuse to tell his story, but to our surprise, he agreed. I stood in the back of the classroom as he spoke and cried through the entire presentation. I had no idea what my parents had endured.

After this speaking engagement, Dad became more open, and he felt comfortable speaking to other gatherings and classrooms. He was interviewed by the Frazier History Museum in Louisville, Kentucky, The National World War II Museum in New Orleans, Louisiana, and by countless students assigned to meet and ask questions of a WWII veteran.

Over the ensuing years, Bob wrote a brief account of his WWII days, attended veteran reunions, and went to Italy with some members of his bomber group to visit their old airfield. In 1998, he had a memorable reunion with five of his crew members. Bob was especially fortunate to fly to the World War II Memorial in Washington, D.C, with other WWII veterans on an Honor Flight.

I asked Dad why he changed his mind and decided to speak about his war experiences. He replied, "People need to know." That was all he said on the subject.

Dad was one of the lucky ones. He came home. He beat his poor chances of survival as a bomber crewman. But the world had changed. Their small town had changed. The terrifying experiences he endured during the war left invisible scars, but he transcended them as he and Frances made a life together, one they never took for granted. They lived their lives to the fullest, relishing every good experience and facing any bad experience with perspective. They had already gone through the worst.

This is their story, told through letters, diaries, writings, interviews, and family memories, with the backdrop of the most destructive conflict in human history. The war had ruled their lives but not their love. Theirs is a story of hope, perseverance, and courage. Through this book, I have shared their story, not only to put a personal face on a significant moment in history and a time of unprecedented change but also to enlighten, engage, and inspire future generations.

Chapter One

Two Families and a Midwestern Town

November 1998

I called ahead and told them a WWII B-17 crewman was coming for a visit. The museum staff was thrilled and asked if they could question him about his experiences during WWII. Dad and I set up a time to visit, and we were ready to go.

Dad was so excited during the four-hour car ride to the National Museum of the United States Air Force in Dayton, Ohio. He talked non-stop about B-17 planes, his job as the radio operator, and his crew. Dad had visited this museum many years before and still remembered where the B-17 plane was located. Spotting the B-17 right away, he quickly made his way toward the large aircraft.

Fifteen feet from the nose of the plane, he suddenly stopped. Standing next to him, I realized he was shaking. I wondered if he was having some kind of medical emergency. His face was white, and his breathing was ragged. Panic! Loathing! Determination! Emotions of fear washed across his face. Then I saw a look of sheer terror glaze over the emotions playing out on his countenance.

He was 22 again, getting up the nerve to climb into that airplane for another bombing mission. Dad was seeing through a portal of time. It was a horrible, terrifying moment of fear and resolution vividly replaying itself. A sinking feeling took over my gut. I didn't know what to do. My strong, steady father was reliving a frightening flashback.

After a few minutes, but what seemed like an eternity, he covered his face with his hands to help block out the memories. Slowly, he regained his composure. His breathing returned to normal. He stopped shaking and calmly walked up to the plane.

We never spoke of it.

June 1936

Fourteen-year-old Bob had just gulped down his breakfast. He hit the screen door running and was down the porch steps of the small house located on the poorer end of Shelby Street in seconds. He yelled, "Goodbye," to his mom, and she replied with her usual, "Bobby, don't go near Silver Creek!" Silver Creek, four blocks east, formed the eastern boundary of New Albany, Indiana. A young boy had died accidentally while playing at Silver Creek several years before, so mothers in town regularly admonished their children not to go there. Normally, Silver Creek would be Bob's destination but not today. He grabbed his bike and took off.

He had a surprisingly expensive bike. His dad had given it to him to help with his paper routes and to eliminate the streetcar fare to and from junior high school. Where the money had come from for such a purchase Bob would never know.

He was soon pedaling out of New Albany and through the town of Clarksville. It was a perfect June day. The sun was shining, and there were no clouds in the sky. Bob kept pedaling until he reached the Second Street Bridge. Also known as the George Rogers Clark Bridge, it spanned the Ohio River and had been built in 1928, when Bob was six years old. He put his hand in the toll collection box pretending to put in a coin. The toll guard did not stop him, and off he went across the bridge into downtown Louisville, Kentucky. Five more miles to go.

Quickly, he pedaled through downtown Louisville. Finally, he was there. He jumped off his bike and looked up into the sky. The eight-mile trip had brought him to his destination, Bowman Field, established just seventeen years earlier in 1919. He had come all this way just to watch the airplanes take off and land. Eastern Airlines and TWA had started flying passenger and mail routes in and out of Bowman Field, so air traffic was picking up at the airport.

Bob Oakes, age 2

A few hours of plane watching were pure rapture for Bob. His parents never dreamed he would ride his bicycle that far from home, and they never found out about his outings to the airport. Such was his love for flying that Bob would risk his secret bicycle ride to Bowman Field just to watch the planes. Flying had captured his heart. He wanted to fly. He wanted to be a pilot. He would stay at the airport as long as he dared before making the eight-mile trek home.

The Oakes Family

Robert "Bob" Tyler Oakes was born on March 21, 1922, in New Albany, Indiana, to Robert A. Oakes and Katie Tyler Oakes. Bob was the youngest of three children. His brother Marvin was eleven years older than Bob, and his sister Wilma was nine years older. Bob was the cute, curly-haired little darling of the Oakes family.

Both of Bob's parents were products of large farm families. They were of a generation that often left the farm to find work in the city. The city, in this instance, was the river town of New Albany, Indiana. Unfortunately, like many other such families, they came without the skills to prosper in a city environment, with only menial, low-paying jobs as a possibility. Even before the Great Depression started in

1929, times were tough. Bob's dad initially did odd jobs, including working as a laborer digging potatoes on nearby farms. He eventually became a motorman on the Interurban, a type of electric railway, with streetcar-like, self-propelled rail cars that ran within and between cities and towns.

Bob as a teenager working on his Uncle's farm.

Bob's mother was the youngest of sixteen children. She graduated from the eighth grade at her small Georgetown, Indiana, school as a top student. The next step in her education should have been to move on to high school. She wanted to continue her education, but she was not allowed to attend. The nearest high school was considered too far away, and her dad did not think a girl should continue school past eighth grade. Sadly, this was not unusual for this era.

Despite their financial position, the Oakes family was a happy, hard-working, close-knit, faith-filled family. Bob's dad led the men's prayer group at the neighborhood Evangelical United Brethren church. The family went to church, as Bob would say, "Every time the doors opened."

As a young boy, Bob played many sports, and his sixth-grade basketball team won the city tournament. He also had two paper routes. His uncles still owned farms, so he would often visit them during the summer, always ready to work there as well as hunt squirrels and rabbits. That experience in shooting would serve him well during his training in gunnery school for the Army. He would later joke, saying that one good thing he learned about working on a farm was that he knew he didn't want to be a farmer.

Cora Martin School basketball team. First row, left to right: John Walts, Leon Bradley, captain Donald Kehoe, William Lee, and Earl Christensen. Second row: James Mann, Robert Oakes, Boner McAfee, Rex Byrd, and Richard Clipp. Back: Robert Graves, coach. Courtesy Robert Graves and Mary Clipp.

The sixth-grade city basketball champs 1934, Cora Martin Elementary. Bob pictured back row second from left.

"I grew up during the Depression," Bob recalled. "I had a lot of fun growing up. Nothing spectacular."

The Brown Family

The Browns lived eight blocks away from the Oakes household in a modest home on Spring Street. Coming from a very poor family, Chester Brown had quit school to work as a caddy at the French Lick Golf Course in French Lick, Indiana, and to deliver telegrams for Western Union. Chester worked his way up the ladder there, eventually becoming the wire chief at the Western Union office in Louisville, Kentucky. Along the way, he met and married Forrest Kegler. The Western Union job was not a high-paying one, but it was enough for Chester, Forrest, and their two children, Chet and Frances, to live comfortably.

In 1940, Chet Brown was a senior at New Albany High School and a local football, track, and basketball star. He and Bob were in the same class, and they became close friends.

Born January 15, 1925, Frances Brown was a social creature, always surrounded by friends. She was a warm and outgoing person, and people loved her. Frances was also a talented athlete, but there were few opportunities available for women to participate in sports. She passed the Red Cross lifeguard course, which was a rare feat for a girl at that time. Frances was also artistic and creative. Among her friends, she set the bar for style with her sewing skills and eye for fashion.

Bob's high school senior picture, 1940.

Frances high school senior picture, 1943.

New Albany High School 1940 Yearbook staff. Bob is fifth from left in the back row.

New Albany, Indiana

New Albany, Indiana, is a town along the Ohio River, a few miles west of Louisville, Kentucky. Founded in 1813 by Joel, Abner, and Nathaniel Scribner, who named the settlement for Albany, New York, it was settled before Indiana became a state in 1816 and is among the earliest towns in Indiana. For a period in the early to mid-1800s, it was also one of the wealthiest. From 1816 to 1860, New Albany was the largest city in Indiana, only to be overtaken in size by Indianapolis, Indiana. Because of its location just below the falls of the Ohio River and near abundant forests, New Albany had a flourishing steamboat-building industry in the mid-1800s, with two famous river boats, *Robert E. Lee* and *Eclipse*, built here. After the collapse of that industry, New Albany segued to other uses of lumber, including plywood, veneer, and baskets, as well as ironworks and glass businesses. In 1940, New Albany had a population of 25,414.

One of the most significant events in New Albany's history started on January 13, 1937, with heavy rains falling for nineteen days on the towns along the Ohio River from Pittsburgh, Pennsylvania, to Cairo, Illinois. The rain and snow came down relentlessly on the Ohio River Valley during the coldest part of winter. The flood waters surged out of the riverbanks and into the surrounding towns and farms. The 1937 flood was the worst recorded flood since traders had first settled along the Ohio River almost two centuries earlier. The waters rose quickly, forcing millions of people along the river to flee their homes. The Red Cross and the Coast Guard were overwhelmed with the enormity of the destruction and the great human need.

Downtown New Albany was quickly submerged under ten feet of rushing water. The river soon surged into residential neighborhoods. New Albany had no fresh water, electricity, phone service, or heat. A massive rescue effort began with private boats and volunteers springing into action to assist the authorities. Fifteen-year-old Bob, who lived in a higher-elevation area of town, was part of this effort, assisting in unloading people from the rescue boats near his home and helping however he could.

During this great flood, when much of the town was still under water, Western Union set up a temporary office at the Brown residence on Spring Street, as the rising water had stopped just a few blocks away. Since people in flooded Indiana towns could not get across the Ohio River to the Western Union in Louisville to send out messages or to receive news, the Brown's home became a satellite office. The homeless and destitute came through the Brown's living room to contact or to hear from their family or friends, making the impromptu telegraph center a very busy place. Chester's wife, Forrest, and their children, Frances and Chet, welcomed their guests and helped to facilitate the running of this important communications hub.

New Albany, IN 1937 Flood

In 1940, New Albany was still dealing with the effects of the Great Depression and the 1937 flood, but times were getting better. A strong sense of family and community emerged out of these disasters. Students had returned to school, shops were open again, and the town took up its familiar existence. The streetcars ran, movie theaters premiered the newest films from Hollywood, and life went on.

Chapter Two

The Dating Game

Beginning in 1939, Frances Brown kept a diary for many years of her life. Her diary entries from these early days give us a glimpse of small-town, Midwestern life before WWII, albeit from a teenage girl's perspective. By including a selection of her entries, I wanted to capture the innocence and excitement of being fifteen in 1940.

Dating in the years before WWII had its own quirks and rules. For Frances and her girlfriends, dating was a popularity competition. The more boys you went out with on a date, the higher your popularity status among your peers. It was not necessarily a matter of attraction or of attachment to someone that counted in the running tally of dates. A date might be going to a movie, a local dance, an athletic event, or for an automobile ride. Frances was a star at this popularity game, sometimes going out on several different dates in one day. She was great fun and had no shortage of offers.

While a girl's success in the dating competition depended on how many guys that you dated or where you were seen, there was a different popularity measurement for men. Material possessions and social status made men more desirable and popular. Having a car, being a star athlete with a varsity sweater, having an enviable talent, and, of course, having the resources to take a girl out somewhere special were all assets in the dating game.

Bob lacked important dating attractions by this standard, as he had little in the way of visible material advantages. However, he had many friends and was liked and respected. Witty and entertaining, he had a reputation for being someone who enjoyed a good time. Still, Frances' popularity may have contributed to his hesitancy in asking her out when he first noticed her.

Bob had a study hall class in the school auditorium. Looking out across the auditorium seats, he spotted Frances Brown. Although she was a freshman, and he was a senior, he later said, "I noticed her, but I didn't have the nerve to ask her out." Of course, that eventually changed.

In 1940, the events of the world could not be completely ignored, but the war news was about countries that seemed far away from peaceful New Albany. No one wanted to dwell on the growing cloud of war. They had lived through the Depression and the devastating flood that had hit New Albany hard in 1937. They had survived. They were young, and life was fun.

With the entries from Frances' diaries that are used in this book, the spelling, grammar, and punctuation have been kept as written by her.

Diary Entry January 1, 1940

Dear Diary,

Today I woke up at 1:10. Peggy and Maxine spent the night. Last night we had a party here and didn't get to bed until 3:00. I had a date with Frank. Dick came up tonight, we played Betty Lue's records for she left them here when she went home last night. Dick left at 10:00 on the dot. Mother said he had to leave then or he couldn't come again. We were going to Club Silver Springs but didn't. I went to bed.

That's All Frances

Diary Entry January 5, 1940

Dear Diary,

Well, as usual, I went to school today. And as it is Friday, it is the last day of the week. Tonight, there was a basketball game. We played Bedford, and we beat them 26-24. Chet made the winning points when the score was 24-24, and one minute, and Chet made a lay-up. Marilyn spent the night. The temperature is 2 below zero.

Frances

Diary Entry January 8, 1940

Dear Diary,

Tonight, Mother, Daddy, and Chet went to the show. Maxine came over to stay with me, and who should walk in the door but Frank and Dick. They didn't leave until 9:30. Boy oh boy did I get him good with a snowball right on the back of the neck, and then I ran into the house, and he couldn't hit me. It was a dirty trick, but I did not want to get hit.

I had a fight with him. He wouldn't give me his pin. It is the greatest thing, but, alas, I didn't get it. Here's hoping I do.

Frances

Diary Entry January 25, 1940

Dear Diary,

Today I got up at 10:00. At 1:00 we went to school and got our report cards. Dick came at 2:30 and we went to see "Dancing Co-ed." It was good with Artie Shaw.

The girls came up tonight—Sylvia, Betty, Marilyn, Peggy, and Maxine. Peggy is spending the night.

We are getting up at 6:00 A.M. to see G.W.T.W. Today I finished reading G.W.T.W.

Frances

Diary Entry January 26, 1940

Dear Diary,

Today Peggy and I got up at 6:45. We caught the 7:00 streetcar and went to Louisville. We were the first there at the show for "Gone with the Wind." We had to stand in line for an hour. Then stayed in the show for an hour until it started! The show was good.

Tonight, we played Hammond and beat them 35-26. What a game! We went to Silver Springs. (Betty and I) Frank said Dick had a date tonight for the dance. Carl and I talked at Silver Springs. I think Carl likes Peggy. Peggy spent the night.

Frances

P.S. Peggy and I just made a great dessert, Marshmallows cut up in a little milk and cooked until melted, good.

Diary Entry February 23,1940

Dear Diary,

Oh, Diary, so much has happened today! First Dick walked home with me and came to the house. Peggy, Lenny, and Paul came up too.

Tonight, Karch was here before the game, and when I went back to call Marilyn, he kissed me.

Frank walked home from Silver Springs. He danced with me too. He broke training, but it was fun. Yes, and then when we were in the kitchen eating, he kissed me. Yes, dear Diary, he did. You could have knocked me over with a feather. He said that he was going to take me to the dance tomorrow, but coach is taking them [the basketball team] to Jeff. He said he would ask Mother if I could go with him Sunday night, but she said no. She thought he was kidding.

Frances

Diary Entry March 2, 1940

Dear Diary,

Today I got up at 10:00 and worked a while. We caught the 2:30 bus for Jeff. We beat Silver Creek. After that I came home. Bob L called and asked for a date for Sunday night. I accepted.

Tonight, we beat Charlestown 43-20. Chet was high point man and Karch was [high point man] this afternoon. Tonight, after the game we went to Silver Springs. I danced with George, Dick, Billy Joe, Victor, and some boy from Jeff. Lonnie walked home with us girls. Betty Lee and Marilyn are spending the night. It is now 12:30.

Frances

Diary Entry April 4, 1940

Dear Diary,

Today Stanley walked home from school with me, after I stayed in for Miss Rockenback for Latin.

I got a photograph album this afternoon.

Tonight, Stanley called from Bob L's and asked me if I could get out of the house for about an hour, and I did. There was Bob L, Betty, Bob B, and Barbara, and guess what!? Stanley said, "Franny dear, would you wear this?" And I said yes, and guess what! It was his "N" [sweater]!!! Oh, happy day. I was supposed to study my Latin for a test, but I didn't.

Frances

Diary Entry April 9,1940

Dear Diary,

Today after school Stanley and Bob L stayed in and got some help from Mr. Thomas for a test for Thursday. They didn't walk home with us.

Bob L asked Bax for a date for Stanley, and they will go with us. Not much else, except Germany invaded Norway and Denmark.

Frances

Diary Entry April 23,1940

Dear Diary,

Today we stayed for the track meet, and it rained all the time. We beat Salem. Stanley and Billy came home with Marilyn and me. Stanley and Billy stayed awhile. Stanley and I got into a fight. It was fun!

We went to Grandma's and got some dandelions. Marilyn and I went to see "Our Town." It was good.

Frances

Bob's shyness was about to fade away. He was cast in the senior play, a production of "Our Town," playing one of the lead characters, George Gibbs. The theater productions at the high school were very good and well attended by the community. Every girl in New Albany High School was swooning over Bob Oakes after his performance in "Our Town." More importantly, it gave this boy from the "wrong part of town" the realization that he had talents. It gave him confidence and a newfound status in the pecking order of high school.

Diary Entry April 26, 1940

Dear Diary,

Today I was elected Queen of the Track Meet [for] tomorrow. This afternoon Stanley and Billy walked home with Betty and I. Then we had to go back to get our pictures taken.

Tonight, I went out with Stanley. I danced with Kay and Billy. Kay asked me if I would go out to the next non-school dance with him, and I told him I thought I would.

We had more fun!

Frances

Diary Entry April 27, 1940

Dear Diary,

Today I was Queen of the track meet, and it was fun. After it was over, we went to Silver Springs. On the way there we were stopped by the Police, and Stanley got a ticket to add to his many troubles.

Tonight, Marilyn and I went up to Betty's. There was Bax and Shine there already. George and Billy were down home with all of us.

My picture was in the paper this afternoon. I got it taken with the winning half mile relay team (Zurschmeade, Kersheral, Zoeller, and Tinnius). They broke the record. We lost the meet though by 2 points.

Not much else. I saw Kay up at Silver Springs, this afternoon.

Frances

Diary Entry May 4, 1940

Dear Diary,

Today I went to the 66th Kentucky Derby with Bax. Oh! It was swell. I got tired though. Chet and Jeanne went with us. Gallahadion won.

Tonight, I had a blind date with Bobby W. We went with Betty and Kay, Nancy and Jack from Indianapolis and Patty and Montana. I had fun.

Frances

In the summer of 1940, Bob and Frances frequented the same places and hung around with the same group of friends. A popular place to hang out was Club Silver Springs. At first, Bob and Frances would casually meet there but that changed to the occasional date. It was a magical summer filled with swimming, horseback riding, dances, tennis, ballgames, hayrides, parties, movies, and hanging out with friends. They often got together to play cards, with pinochle, bridge, and poker being the favorites. Frances and her group of girlfriends would get together to knit, and, of course, to talk about boys. Dancing to the great swing music of their time was very popular, and they often taught each other new dance moves and tried them out at Silver Springs.

Diary Entry June 1, 1940

Dear Diary,

Today I washed my hair in the afternoon. Tonight, I went to Nancy's and Betty's dance. I had oodles of fun. Guess what! I danced with Chet! We jitterbugged and had more fun!

Chet, Frank, Karch, and Miller crashed the dance.

Frances

Diary Entry June 10, 1940

Dear Diary,

Today the paper hanger came and papered the hall. Tonight, Marilyn Betty, Sylvia, and I went to see "Black Beauty Rides Again." Then we went to Silver Springs.

Chet and Jeanne are going steady again. Chet danced with Lettie in Silver Springs.

I think Stanley and I are splitting up.

Frances

Then, Chet brought his friend, Bob Oakes, home for the first time. Their parents were out, and Frances was cooking a meal of fried chicken, mashed potatoes, green beans, and gravy. Maybe Frances was a little nervous, as her gravy came out like school paste! It was terrible, verging on inedible, but Bob ate it anyway.

Diary Entry June 11, 1940

Dear Diary,

This morning I worked, and then I laid out in the sun. Betty and I went to Emery's to get ice cream cones. We went to Silver Springs and met up with Johnny and Bob Oakes. We all went riding with Jerry and Chas in their car. More fun!

Frances

Diary Entry June 14, 1940

Dear Diary,

Today, I got up early and worked, and this afternoon I did the same. Tonight, I had a date with Johnny. We met Oakes at Silver Springs without a date. He was supposed to have one, and we went and got Marilyn.

We stayed at her house awhile and then came here, and fried eggs. Oh boy! What fun!

Frances

Frances and her friends walked everywhere. They walked downtown. They walked to and from school. They walked to their friends' houses. They walked to ball games. They walked to Emery's Ice Cream Shop. They walked to Silver Springs. Having a car or going for a car ride was a rare luxury.

Diary Entry June 24, 1940

Dear Diary,

I got up at 11:15 after getting in about 1:30 last night. This afternoon we went to the show and saw "Lincoln in Illinois" with Raymond Massey. We got out at 5:25. Tonight we went to Marilyn's and met George, Johnny, and Byrd and went back to Marilyn's. Then we all walked to Silver Springs. I danced with Karch, and he took us all home and had nine in the car. Virgil, Johnny, Bob Oakes, George, Karch, Marilyn, Wanda, Sylvie, and I were all in the car. I sat in the front.

Frances

Diary Entry June 27, 1940

Dear Diary,

Today I spent the day out at the Country Club with the rest of the girls. We took our own lunch.

Tonight, I had a Sub Deb [a local teen sorority] meeting here at home. We are going to have an Indian Dance. Oh! What a cute idea.

Wendel Willkie was just nominated for President for the Republicans. Not much else.

Frances

Diary Entry June 28, 1940

Dear Diary,

Today we went swimming. Tonight, George and Bill stopped in, and then Bennie and Sylvia came before we went riding, Oakes was with us too. We had a flat tire up on the highway at 10:30. At 11:20 Mr. Wiedershein came after us after we called him. The boys needed to get tire patching, so we drove to Jeff and got some. We left them there fixing the tire because they didn't want to go home. That's all. It's 12:15 now.

Frances

Diary Entry July 24, 1940

Dear Diary,

Today I got up at Marilyn's. Sylvia and I caught the 9:30 bus. I worked when I got home. This afternoon I slept off and on. I went to Anna's dance with Bud tonight. Had fun.

I danced for a while with my shoes off. It was fun.

Frances

Diary Entry August 22, 1940

Dear Diary,

Today Mother went to a funeral and left me alone all morning. This afternoon I washed my hair and started knitting on the right side of the front of my sweater. I think I'll finish it tonight.

Silvia and Marilyn came up tonight and later George and Bill. We just stayed here at home. Waited with Marilyn and Silvia for the bus. Ebby called tonight for a date tomorrow night. We are going with Dorothy and George. Johnny called me too, darn. I had already accepted Ebby.

Frances

Diary Entry August 28, 1940

Dear Diary,

Today I took the car out for the first time, and did I have fun. I drove out to the Colonial Club and then I went swimming.

Tonight, Bax came over and we went to Aunt Bonnie's home, came home and ate.

Frances

Diary Entry September 4, 1940

Dear Diary,

Today I slept until 11:30. This afternoon I drove to Hamburg and back. It was an 18-mile trip.

Tonight, I went on a scavenger hunt and a wienie roast with George. We went with Johnny and Peggy, Don and Maxine. We had fun and we won a blow gun for the prize.

I got home at 11:00.

Frances

Diary Entry September 5, 1940

Dear Diary,

Today I got up and helped clean the house for Chet's party. Chet and I went downtown this afternoon, and I got a pair of shoes. Chet went to Louisville to get a pair of shoes.

I went to a dance and had lots of fun. Bob Oakes took me.

Frances

Friends and relatives dropped by Frances' house frequently, often just to use the telephone. Of course, anyone who showed up around mealtime was invited to stay and eat. It was a time of fun and few worries. Bob and Frances were just part of the group who hung around together, and then something happened.

On September 6, 1940, Frances wrote, "Dear Diary, Bob left this morning for Purdue and it does seem like he's gone. I don't know what we'll do now." On September 10, she received the first of many letters Bob sent while attending Purdue.

Diary Entry September 10, 1940

Dear Diary,

Today we went to school, and we stayed all day. Marilyn, Sylvia, and I went downtown after school.

Mother and Daddy came home from taking Chet to Muncie [Ball State College].

Bobby S called and asked for a date tonight. I had lessons, so I gave him one for Sunday night.

I got a card from Bob Oakes, and I wrote him a letter.

Frances

Diary Entry September 24, 1940

Dear Diary,

Today I saw Johnny once at lunch outside. This afternoon Dick stopped in for a while and stayed for supper.

Stanley called tonight and we got everything straightened out.

Bobby S called and asked for a date for Friday night, but I have one with Stanley.

Frances

I got a letter from Oakes--three pages.

I wish Johnny had asked me before now because now I couldn't go with him.

Diary Entry September 30, 1940

Dear Diary,

Today I saw Johnny, at noon out on the grass at school. After school I wrote Oakes a letter, and tonight I got my lessons.

Dick dropped in and borrowed my music piece "The Nearness of You." Louisville won the American League from Kansas City tonight 3-0.

Frances

Diary Entry October 10, 1940

Dear Diary,

Today after school Bax and I went to Louisville. I got some Charles of the Ritz lipstick and powder. She got a skirt shortened.

Tonight, I went to Sub Debs. Johnny called when I got back. Johnny found out that he's not going to the country Saturday.

Frances

Diary Entry October 27, 1940

Dear Diary,

Today I went to church and Sunday school. And then, I helped Mother fix dinner. Jeanne came. Chet left to go back to school around 3:00. Bill and I and Byrd went up to Marilyn's.

Then we all went up to the Power Plant. Tonight, we went to Louisville and saw Cab Calloway. He was swell. Chet got back to school at 3:30 this morning.

Frances

Diary Entry November 10, 1940

Dear Diary,

Today I went to church and Sunday school, and then I stayed home until 3:45.

Then we went to the show and saw "Down Argentina Way." It was good.

Frances

Marilyn is spending the night because it is too bad to go home because of the rain. She got Byrd's sweater, his white one with the red "N."

Diary Entry December 4, 1940

Dear Diary,

Today we got our second six weeks report grades, and I got History C+, Latin C, Geometry A, Gym A, English B+.

Frances

Diary Entry December 9, 1940

Dear Diary,

After school there was a called Bel Canto [high school singing group] meeting, and we are going to sell "Bundles for Britain" tags.

Mother made some divinity fudge tonight.

Frances

Diary Entry December 22, 1940

Dear Diary,

Today I wore my new clothes to Church and Sunday school, and after that Daddy and I washed the dog and he looks so nice and clean. This afternoon I was in the program at Church and tonight too. Afterwards we went up to Silver Springs and I saw Oakes.

Frances

Diary Entry December 24, 1940

Dear Diary,

Today I slept till 10:00 and then I got up and helped Mother wrap packages. I helped clean up the house, and then this afternoon I slept a while.

Chet got home at 6:30, and he brought Jeanne. We all went out to Grandma Brown's and Grandma Kegler's and Aunt LaVelle's for eggnog.

Frances

Diary Entry December 26, 1940

Dear Diary,

I slept till 11:30 then at 1:30 I went to Peggy's to play bridge. Tonight, I went with a group to Silver Springs and saw Oakes. We danced then went to the Cottage. Oakes asked me for a date, but Herman had called first.

Frances

Diary Entry December 29, 1940

Dear Diary,

Today Chet and I went to church and Sunday school, and then afterwards I bugged. This afternoon I taught Gene the "Richmond." Dick and Bob L stayed for supper.

Tonight, Mother and Daddy and I went to Aunt Bonnie's after supper. We came home to listen to President Roosevelt's speech.

Frances

When Bob came home from Purdue that December, at the end of his first semester, he started hanging around with the group again. He soon asked Frances for a date. No surprise, she was all booked up, but he did manage to get a few dates with her. Frances kept a list of her dates in her diary. There are 97 dates listed for the year 1940. Bob Oakes only appears twice on that list.

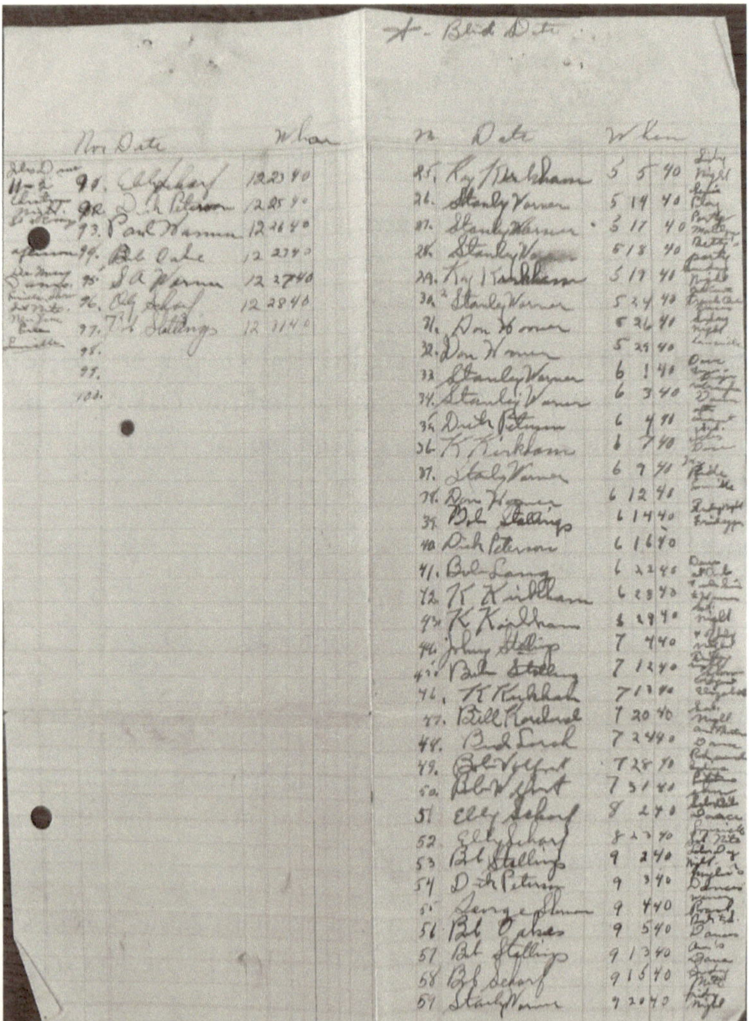
* - Blind Date

No.	Date	When
91.	Elly Scharf	12 23 40
92.	Dick Peterson	12 25 40
93.	Paul Warman	12 26 40
94.	Bob Oake	12 27 40
95.	S A Warman	12 27 40
96.	Elly Scharf	12 28 40
97.	7? Stallings	12 31 40
98.		
99.		
100.		

No.	Date	When
25.	Ky Kirkham	5 5 40
26.	Stanley Warner	5 14 40
27.	Stanley Warner	5 11 40
28.	Stanley Warner	5 18 40
29.	Ky Kirkham	5 17 41
30.	Stanley Warner	5 24 40
31.	Don Warner	5 26 41
32.	Don Warner	5 25 40
33.	Stanley Warner	6 1 40
34.	Stanley Warner	6 3 40
35.	Dick Peterson	6 4 41
36.	K Kirkham	6 7 40
37.	Stanley Warner	6 9 41
38.	Don Warner	6 12 41
39.	Bob Stallings	6 14 40
40.	Dick Peterson	6 16 40
41.	Bob Lang	6 22 40
42.	K Kirkham	6 23 40
43.	K Kirkham	6 29 40
44.	Johny Stallings	7 4 40
45.	Bob Stalling	7 12 40
46.	K Kirkham	7 13 40
47.	Bill Rowland	7 20 40
48.	Bud L[illegible]k	7 24 40
49.	Bob Volfert	7 28 40
50.	Bob Wolfert	7 31 40
51	Elly Scharf	8 2 40
52	Elly Scharf	8 23 40
53	Bob Stallings	9 2 40
54	Dick Peterson	9 3 40
55	George [illegible]	9 4 40
56	Bob Oakes	9 5 40
57	Bob Stallings	9 13 40
58	Bob Scharf	9 15 40
59	Stanley Warner	9 20 40

Page 1 of Frances' tally of dates for the year 1940.

Frances, age 16, in 1940 behind her parent's home.

Back row left to right. Frances, Marilyn, Maxine.
Front row left to right. Sylvia, Peggy

Chapter Three

Bob's A Darling!

Frances Brown would be sixteen on January 15, 1941. She started her 1941 diary with a clarification of the diary's purpose.

Diary Entry January 1, 1941

Dear Dairy,

I have chosen you as my means of keeping track of the events of 1941. My dates, places I go, what I do, and if I have fun or not. I'll try to keep you well informed and up to date. I shall take you with me wherever I go for a vacation. I hope at the end of the year, I shall have filled each page. Here's to better times for us in 1941.

Yours Truly,

Frances Brown

Diary Entry January 3, 1941

Dear Diary,

Today I saw Johnny at school at noon. He asked me for a date for Saturday night, and I have one. He makes the third person that asked me for a date for Saturday. I was so mad.

At 5:00 the basketball team left for Bedford and they beat us 33-31. Bob Oakes and I went to the Sub Deb dinner tonight and we went with Bud and Peggy. Had fun.

Chet went to Bedford to see the game. The Western Union asked Chet to describe the Notre Dame game tomorrow night with Kentucky for the ticker.

Frances

Diary Entry January 15, 1941

Dear Diary,

Today being my 16th birthday, Daddy gave me an extra dollar on my allowance, and Grandma Brown gave me some money. Aunt Bonnie left me some money up at Grandma Kegler's.

After school we went to Bel Canto and then to my house. Bax caught the bus home. I went to Choir practice at church tonight and got my lessons. The basketball team left around 12:00 noon for Greencastle. They are going to spend the night.

Frances

P.S. I wrote Oakes a letter after I finished studying.

Diary Entry January 16th, 1941

Dear Diary,

Today we only went 3 periods of school Mr. Katterjohn [the principal] asked the Sub Debs to usher at graduation tomorrow night. The club ate downtown at noon and then went to the show. We saw "The Hit Parade of 1941." It was awful. Tonight, we saw "Northwest Mounted Police." It was good.

I got a birthday card from Oakes. I almost fell over for what it said.

Frances

Diary Entry January 25, 1941

Dear Diary,

Today Marilyn and I sold "Infantile Paralysis" tags from 10:00 to 11:30. Made $3.00.

This afternoon I slept. Tonight, Oakes and I went to the basketball game. Washington beat us 47-27, I think. Oakes got the car and we took Maxine and Barr to Emery's with us to get ice cream. We went to The Cottage. We had fun.

Frances

Diary Entry January 26, 1941

Dear Diary,

Today I went to church and Sunday school. I sang in the choir at church.

Went out with Bob Oakes at 7:40. We had fun. Went to Silver Springs. We saw Stanley and he had the car, too. Coming up Spring Street tonight a fellow ran into us making a left-hand turn. He didn't stop, and we were not going fast enough to catch him. He dented the front right bumper.

Frances

Diary Entry January 29, 1941

Dear Diary,

Today we had a small Pep Session for the Jeff game tonight. We beat them 26-22. The school got off from 11:45 to 1:45 to see the National Guards off for Mississippi.

Tonight, I saw Bob Oakes at Silver Springs. He quit school and got a job at DuPonts. Isn't that awful?

Well, that's all.

Frances

Attending Purdue University was a dream come true for Bob. With his mechanical and analytical talents, Purdue was a perfect fit for Bob. He loved his time there and remained a Purdue man all his life. But reality had hit. He did not have the resources to continue his education at Purdue. He would have to come home and work to save enough money to go back to Purdue. His older siblings, Marvin and Wilma, had worked their way through college, becoming teachers. Bob would have to get his college education the same way.

Diary Entry February 26, 1941

Dear Diary,

Today we had a final French test, and it wasn't so hard. I think it was the easiest final I ever took. I went to Bel Canto after school.

Tonight, Virgil stopped by and so did Dick. Then we went walking in the snow and stopped at Silver Springs. Marilyn asked Byrd for tomorrow night.

Frances

P.S. Bob Oakes called and wanted a date for Sunday night. I already had one, so we are going out Sunday afternoon.

Diary Entry March 2, 1941

Dear Diary,

Today I went to church and Sunday school, and then I got my lessons. This afternoon I had a date with Bob Oakes. Dick and Betty went with us, and we went to Louisville and saw a show.

Tonight, Bob S and I went to Jeff and saw a show. I got in at 11:50.

That's all.

Frances

Diary Entry April 4, 1941

Dear Diary,

Today after school we went bowling. I beat them all.

Tonight, Virgil came by and Sylvia and Peggy came up, we played bridge. Then we went to Silver Springs and The Cottage, and I got to drive home from The Cottage.

Frances

Diary Entry April 18, 1941

Dear Diary,

Today at school we had the Science Club Program.

Tonight, I had a date with Bob Oakes, and we met Bax and Shorty at The Cottage. Then we all went riding in the car and listened to the radio.

Then we came home. Bob was so cute, the way he acted and all.

Frances

Diary Entry April 27, 1941

Dear Diary,

Today I went to church and Sunday school, and then Virgil and I bowled two games.

This afternoon Maxine and Sylvia and I went walking, and then Sylvia went home and Bob Oakes and Neal walked down home with us.

Tonight, Oakes and I went out with Neal and Betty. We went to Silver Springs and The Cottage and listened to the radio at 10:30.

Frances

The initial tally of dates with Bob Oakes was small. In April 1941, Bob Oakes was listed four times out of twelve dates on Frances' date list for that month, but Bob's name kept showing up more frequently. She was beginning to take more notice of this guy.

Diary Entry May 3, 1941

Dear Diary,

Today the boys got up and left around 11:00 for the Derby, Whirlaway won the Derby, and Chet won some money.

Tonight, I had a date with Oakes. We went to a sorority dance at the C's. Had a swell time.

Frances

Diary Entry May 9, 1941

Dear Diary,

Today nothing much happened at school. Today after school I went downtown, and I got a pair of jodhpurs [pants for horseback riding].

Tonight, I had a date with Bob Oakes. We saw the class play. It was grand.

Frances

Bob looked nice.

Diary Entry May 18, 1941

Dear Diary,

Today I went to church and Sunday school. Tonight, I had a date with Oakes. Tyler and Shine went with us. We saw "The Road to Zanzibar" with Bob Hope and Bing Crosby. It was good.

Frances

Diary Entry May 21, 1941

Dear Diary,

Today after school I went to Bel Canto and then Bax, Tyler, and I went for a walk. Tonight, I went to church Choir Practice, and then Oakes came up and helped me with my final Geometry test.

Frances

P.S. I made an A!

Diary Entry May 25, 1941

Dear Diary,

Mother and Dad and I walked over to the park. I watched Oakes and Pat play tennis. They walked home with me, and Oakes helped me with Geometry.

Oakes came over tonight and we read and looked at pictures and then we went to Silver Springs.

Frances

Diary Entry May 29, 1941

Dear Diary,

Today the paper hanger came and papered the kitchen and the breakfast room. Tonight, Bob came by. Betty came down. We got Shine at the park and we all walked up to Silver Springs.

I got Bob's ring, and he has mine.

Betty and I got to bed at 12:30. We talked for a long time.

Frances

Bob and Frances had exchanged their high school class rings. The exchanging of class rings was a definite sign that the relationship had developed to a new level. It did not necessarily mean complete exclusivity in dating, but this was considered a step on the way to a long-term relationship and signaled that they were an "item." In May 1941, Bob was listed twelve times out of sixteen on Frances' dates list for the month.

Diary Entry June 7, 1941

Dear Diary,

Today, the gang went on a picnic, and I had a swell time.

Frances

P.S. Bob's a darling!

Just as Bob and Frances were becoming a serious item, life took another turn.

Diary Entry June 22, 1941

Dear Diary,

Bob said tonight that next week he might have to go to Birmingham or Denver or West Virginia, or get fired.

Frances

P.S. I don't know what I'll do.

Diary Entry June 23, 1941

From left to right: Peaches Browning, Marilyn Baxter, Frances, and Bob.

Dear Diary,

Today I worked all morning helping Mother. This afternoon I drove up to Betty's. Sylvia and Nancy Lee were there, and we played bridge.

Tonight, Mom and Dad took me down to State Street Park to watch Bob play ball. Then he and I went out. We didn't go in any place because he looked awful (he said). So, we stayed here till 11:30, and he went home.

Frances

Diary Entry June 24, 1941

Dear Diary,

Today, Nancy Lee, Bax, Sylvia, Betty, and I went horseback riding. I rode the horse named Dan and had a grand time.

Tonight, Bob bought two new tires and spent the night putting them on. Around 9:45 he came by to tell me about tomorrow night.

Guess that's all.

Frances

Diary Entry June 25, 1941

Dear Diary,

Today, Bax, Sylvia, Peggy, and I went swimming.

Bob said tonight that he was going to Birmingham. He's supposed to go to work in Birmingham Monday morning. That means he won't be here Sunday.

That's all.

Frances

Diary Entry June 26, 1941

Dear Diary,

Today I ironed for Mother. Then I went with Sylvia and Mary Lee to the pool. We swam all afternoon.

Tonight, I went to Sub Deb and Bob came after me.

Bob promised that I could have anything I wanted, and I told him red roses Saturday night, and he said, "OK." I wish he didn't have to go Sunday to Alabama.

Frances

P.S. Shine called Bob "Little Acorn." I think that's cute.

Diary Entry June 27, 1941

Dear Diary,

Today I got up and didn't do much. Chet gave me a half dollar for nothing at all.

This afternoon Barb had a bridge party. I won first prize, a charm bracelet. Tonight, Bob, Dick, Bax, and I went to Louisville to the Derby Inn.

Bob got awful sleepy tonight, and so we came home.

He doesn't want to go to Birmingham at all, and I don't want him to.

Frances

Diary Entry June 28, 1941

Dear Diary,

This afternoon Sylvia and I went out to the Club, and we stayed all afternoon.

Bob worked all day today and stopped by to call his dad to come and get him because it was raining.

Tonight, Bob and I went to Louisville to the show. We saw Bob Hope in "Caught in the Draft." It was swell. And we saw "San Antonia Rose," and it was good too.

Guess that's all.

Frances

Diary Entry June 29, 1941

Dear Diary,

Today Chet and I got in the car to go to Silver Springs, and we couldn't get it started, so we missed Silver Springs. Bob was supposed to come over for dinner, but he had to go to Milltown with his folks. He flew a plane out there for 15 minutes.

Tonight, Bob and I went out.

Frances

Diary Entry June 30, 1941

Dear Diary,

This morning Chet and I washed the dog. This afternoon Bob, Dick, Bax, and I went swimming at the Colonial Club and horseback riding. Bob, Dick, and Bax came for supper, and then we went out. I gave Bob my Sub Deb pin. He and Pat didn't leave until 1:30. He didn't want to leave at all for Alabama. I know I didn't want him to go.

I asked Stanley to go to the hayride tomorrow night since Bob is leaving tomorrow.

Frances

On Frances' June 1941 date list, Bob Oakes was listed seventeen out of 21 dates. Now he was leaving, and their long-distance correspondence began again. When Bob could, he came home to New Albany to see his family, friends, and Frances. She continued to date and go out with her friends.

Diary Entry July 7, 1941

Dear Diary,

Today I got a 5-1/2page letter from Bob, and was I glad to hear from him. This afternoon I mailed him a letter. Then I went swimming with Sylvia.

Tonight, I went with Virgil to see "The Chocolate Soldier." It was good. There were six of us who went.

Guess that's all.

Frances

Diary Entry July 15, 1941

Dear Diary,

Today Bax and I fixed Dr. Baxter dinner, and then we went swimming. I wrote Bob a letter and took a nap.

At 7:00 Betty, Sylvia, and I went horseback riding, and I rode Dart. I had a marvelous time.

When I got back Martha and I went to the show. We saw "Philadelphia Story." It was grand.

Frances

Diary Entry July 27, 1941

Dear Diary,

Today around 10:30 Bob came over and he helped us wash the dog. This afternoon Shine and Betty went with us, and we rode all around the country. Oakes got sleepy, and I drove from Utica to the Country Club.

Tonight, we went to Louisville and rode around Louisville. Then Bob and I stopped at the Cottage for about 45 minutes and came home. He left around 1:00. Bob leaves for Birmingham in the morning.

That's all.

Frances

Diary Entry August 25, 1941

Dear Diary,

Today I got up around 10:00 and got a letter from Bob. He's coming home this weekend.

This afternoon Sylvia and I met Maxine out at the club. Tonight, I drove Mom and Dad out to Warner's to get some eggs.

Frances

I got a card from Bob this afternoon.

Diary Entry August 30, 1941

Dear Diary,

Today I got up and cleaned the house. I went swimming and played tennis at the Colonial Club.

Tonight, I had a date with Oakes. George and Peggy went with us. We went to Fountaine Ferry [local amusement park]. I rode the Racing Derby. I about broke my neck.

Frances

Diary Entry August 31, 1941

Dear Diary,

Today I got up and went to church and Sunday school.

Tonight, Bax, Pete, Shine, and Betty went with Oakes and I to see "Dr Jekyll and Mr. Hyde." It was grand and horrifying.

Frances

Diary Entry September 5, 1941

Dear Diary,

Today Chet and I went downtown and then Mom and I went to Louisville. We ordered a fur coat. I got a new skirt and we got home at 4:30.

Gussie, Betty Stocker and I went to the show and saw "Sun Valley Serenade." It was good.

Frances

P.S. I got an 8 page letter from Bob.

P.P.S. I smoked a cigarette.

Diary Entry November 19, 1941

Dear Diary,

Bob came home today for good. We went to the Pep Rally tonight!

Frances

At age sixteen and a sophomore in high school, there was now only one name on Frances' date list for November 1941, and that was Bob Oakes. Frances had only two more diary entries for the year.

Diary Entry December 7, 1941

Dear Diary,

Japan bombed Hawaii and the Philippines today.

Diary Entry December 8, 1941

Today the U.S. declared war on Japan.

Chapter Four

Life Takes a Different Course

In 1942, Frances would turn seventeen in January, and Bob would turn 20 in March.

Their lives would soon be forever changed, but at first the impact felt negligible to them.

Bob recalled, "When the war first broke out after Pearl Harbor, we heard about it but didn't think much about it. Later that day I was on a double date [with Frances], going to a movie showing at Loew's Theater [now The Louisville Palace] in Louisville. I thought, well, we're going into war. We have to get it over with, do what you have to do to get the job done."

In the interlude between the declaration of war and Bob leaving for military service, Bob and Frances spent the rest of the year cramming in all the activities of their youth that would fall away around them.

Over time, the war that seemed so far away crept into their lives, as it did for everyone on the home front. The seriousness and unknowns of the future began to hang over all they did. Their youth, the ramifications of the war, and the changes to the country and the world would certainly be different than any generation before or after.

As war correspondent Ernie Pyle observed, "...you realized vividly how everybody in America has changed, how everyday life suddenly stopped and suddenly began again on a different course."

The attack on Pearl Harbor was the catalyst that changed popular opinion about going to war. Before the Pearl Harbor attack, 80 percent of Americans were reluctant to join the battle. For years, the United States had watched from the side lines as the brutal expansion of the Nazi Reich in Europe and North Africa spread. They had watched the Japanese take over Indonesia and islands in the Pacific. The final tipping point that propelled the United States into WWII was the attack on Pearl Harbor. It was the end of the world that Americans knew and the beginning of an unknown future. The whole world was at war, and the United States had finally been drawn into the conflict.

After the Pearl Harbor attack, there was widespread fear of German submarine attacks along the Atlantic coast and Japanese attacks along the Pacific coast. If the Japanese could bomb Hawaii, could they attack the United States mainland? The country was woefully unprepared to defend itself. Americans asked themselves, "What will happen next?"

It is hard for us to fathom the depth of stress and anxiety that Americans endured through the war. Everyone was affected. Everyone had a father, a son, a husband, a brother, an uncle, a relative, or a friend in the military. When the United States entered the war, the Axis powers were winning decisively all around the world. The situation did not look promising for the Allies.

The first and most obvious change was the number of men and women entering wartime service. The American workforce was profoundly impacted, as approximately 20 percent of male workers entered military service. Every sector of employment—education, sales, repair work, service industries, medical, and many more—lost men to the military. Familiar faces were missing throughout the nation, including the town of New Albany, where 2,999 men enlisted.

Many women also entered military service, and even more joined the defense workforce. As the United States shifted into war mode, women stepped into war production jobs vacated by men leaving for the war. Paul McNutt (former governor of Indiana), head of the War

Manpower Commission, remarked, "Women have shown that they can do, or learn to do, almost any kind of work."

As the United States entered WWII, Frances was a junior in high school. After graduating from high school, she started college at Indiana University, but when Bob was shipped to the front for combat, she dropped out of school to work at an Army facility that shipped out supplies. Her plans for a college education and a career were put on hold.

Even something as routine as weather reports changed with the war. Detailed weather reports, weather maps in the papers, and maps in public places were forbidden. There were no more reports of cold or warm fronts moving across the country, no statistics on wind patterns and barometric pressures. The government wanted to prevent any potential enemy from obtaining weather information that would aid in planning an attack.

The government's concerns were not unfounded. There was a very real enemy presence along the Atlantic and Pacific coasts and in the Gulf of Mexico. On December 20, 1941, Japanese submarines began attacking American oil tankers along the California coast. Some attacks occurred within sight of people on shore. At the same time, German submarines began operating off the East Coast and the Gulf of Mexico. They were intent on sinking merchant ships, sometimes within sight of land, making Americans first-hand witnesses to the war.

How long would it be before the enemies directed their attacks directly at the mainland? The news was bad on all fronts. On Christmas 1941, Hong Kong fell to the Japanese. By February 1941, the Navy reported that almost 50 merchant ships had been sunk or damaged by enemy submarines operating on the United States coast and 438 merchant sailors had been lost. By April, the number of merchant vessels sunk by enemy submarines had risen to 200.

With the increase of disturbing war setbacks, especially in the Pacific, Americans sought escape in the movie theaters. Attendance was up and the realities of the war could be forgotten for a few hours, except that movie theaters were also a source of news about the war. Since there were no home televisions, newsreels at the movie theaters provided a visual of the conflicts around the world, helping the war to become more real to Americans who were oceans away from the battles.

Meanwhile, other big changes began to envelop the country. Since the United States had entered the war late, there was much catching up to do. An army must be fed, clothed, and armed. American manufacturing and industry shifted to wartime production of military goods instead of consumer goods. This caused shortages and rationing for the American public. Wars demand a great deal of sacrifice from civilians, and this was true for the American people on the home front.

The disruption of trade caused limited availability of some goods. With Japan's conquest of many rubber suppliers in the Pacific, rubber shortages became a reality These were markets that had previously been open to the United States. Compared with most countries, the United States was rich in natural resources and had been supplying military resources to the Allies, especially England, since the beginning of the conflict. The United States continued to send supplies and food both during and after the war to people in war-ravaged areas in Europe.

In May 1942, the Roosevelt administration created the Office of Price Administration (OPA), and rationing books were distributed to every household in the States. Local boards oversaw and controlled rationing on the local levels. This was the great equalizer. It was not how rich you were but, rather, how large your family was that determined how many rationing stamps a family received. The OPA rationed automobiles, tires, gas, fuel oil, coal, firewood, nylon, silk, shoes, typewriters, bicycles, rubber footwear, and stoves.

Rationed foods included bacon, butter, sugar, meat, dairy products, eggs, coffee, dried fruits, jams, jellies, lard, shortening, cooking oils, and canned fish. Not surprisingly, sugar became among the most greatly prized commodities. Americans were encouraged to plant "victory gardens" for growing and canning their own vegetables and fruits. This not only helped families to feed themselves but also freed up factories for military food production.

Each family's ration book contained stamps that had to be used when buying a rationed commodity. The amount of ration stamps given to a family not only depended on the size of the family but also on the type of family members. For instance, households with babies were allowed to purchase canned milk, a commodity that was shipped to the military and not available for regular consumption.

Other items besides those being rationed also became scarce. For example, the Army received 50 to 70 percent of America's wool, as the rapidly expanding military had to be clothed. Americans bought up all the commodities they could whenever they could. Not surprisingly, hoarding and black marketing of essential items occurred. Barter systems developed as well. Food could be used as money to trade for needed commodities and for services rendered.

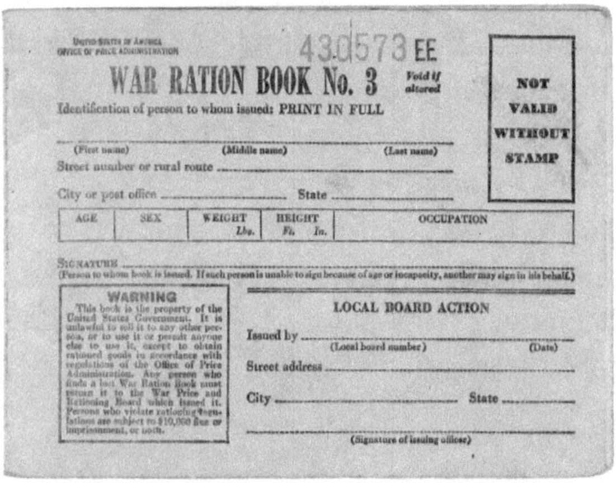

UNITED STATES OF AMERICA
OFFICE OF PRICE ADMINISTRATION

430573 EE

WAR RATION BOOK No. 3

Void if altered

Identification of person to whom issued: PRINT IN FULL

(First name) (Middle name) (Last name)

Street number or rural route ....

City or post office .... State ....

AGE	SEX	WEIGHT Lbs.	HEIGHT Ft. In.	OCCUPATION

SIGNATURE ....
(Person to whom book is issued. If such person is unable to sign because of age or incapacity, another may sign in his behalf.)

NOT VALID WITHOUT STAMP

WARNING
This book is the property of the United States Government. It is unlawful to sell it to any other person, or to use it or permit anyone else to use it, except to obtain rationed goods in accordance with regulations of the Office of Price Administration. Any person who finds a lost War Ration Book must return it to the War Price and Rationing Board which issued it. Persons who violate rationing regulations are subject to $10,000 fine or imprisonment, or both.

LOCAL BOARD ACTION

Issued by ....
(Local board number) (Date)

Street address ....

City .... State ....

....
(Signature of issuing officer)

United States ration book

Besides rationing, other activities were curtailed. An empty metal toothpaste tube had to be turned in to get a new tube of toothpaste.

In June 1942, the manufacturing of metal office furniture, radios, phonographs, refrigerators, vacuum cleaners, washing machines, and sewing machines for civilian purchase ceased.

Car racing and driving for sightseeing were banned. The speed limit for driving was reduced to 35 miles per hour everywhere, and the number of automobile tires you could own was reduced to five per family. Rubber was in great demand, as its availability had been drastically reduced. Less driving and slower driving helped to conserve rubber as well as fuel. Consumer car sales ended in January 1942. The reductions in automobile-related commodities were especially difficult for a car-loving American public who relished the freedom and convenience automobiles provided.

All these measures affected Frances' and Bob's families. Their friends and relatives were also under the same rationing and changes to life. Like most Americans, they adapted to the changes and supported the war effort. The effect of this massive effort to raise, train, and supply the military was to pull the nation together in a united cause.

Because of this effort, the United States produced the best armed and trained military in history. Production lines replenished lost equipment and spent ammunition. Once in full swing, the American manufacturing of war goods outpaced all other countries. The might and resolve of the American people reached a zenith that no other country could touch. Isolated from the conflict and operating in a safe environment, the wartime effort in the United States had little to slow it down. The joint sacrifices and resolve of the American military and American civilians eventually paid off in victory on both war fronts.

Chapter Five

Be A Gold Digger

Bob enlisted, instead of being drafted, into the United States Army Air Force on September 22, 1942. He had dreamed of being a pilot since he was a young boy, so he chose the Army Air Force to ensure he would fly. Bob's passion for flying had led to some pilot training before he enlisted, but he had not logged enough hours for a pilot's license. He had also managed to get a job at Bowman Field in Louisville as a surveyor so that he could be around airplanes.

On the home front, Bob and Frances realized they were in love and decided they were meant for each other. Besides the problem of their pending separation by war, they were met with opposition from Frances' mother and many of Frances' friends. In 1943, she was a senior in high school and planning on attending college. Bob was three years older than Frances, with no career, no higher education degree, and little to offer her. Now they were caught in a world at war, but they continued to hope for their future.

After being called to active duty on January 28, 1943, Bob was shipped to Sheppard Field [now Sheppard Air Force Base] near Wichita Falls, Texas, for basic training. Frances and Bob wrote to each other almost every day that he was deployed. She kept all his letters, many of which are found throughout this book. Sadly, Frances' letters to Bob were lost during the war.

The following letters represent expressions of Bob's feelings for Frances and his experiences as an enlisted airman in WWII. The spelling, punctuation, and grammar have been kept intact.

---·--/ -···-/·-·/·-··/··/-·/--·/

January 31, 1943

My Darling Frances,

I finally have a bed and a roof to live under. We arrived here at Shepherd Field at about 2:00 P.M. We were on the train for 35 hours.

I have found out why we were called so soon. Instead of waiting our time in civilian life we wait as a special private in the regular army. In the meantime, we take our basic training which consists of drill and calisthenics. We also get the private pay of $50.00 a month. Of course, all of this brought on plenty of griping from all. None of us like it, if course. But all we can do is wait till our cadet training starts.

As yet they have not issued us uniforms, but we hope they will soon, as we are running out of clean clothes fast.

It's going to be hard on this old man being so far away from you. But if you'll just keep me showered with letters, I think, I'll make out O.K. It's going to be a long time before I see you again. But when I do, I hope you haven't changed a bit, and I hope you love me more than ever. If they don't keep me too busy, I'll write to you every day. I would like to have a picture of you. If you'll do this, I'll kiss you when I get back, love.

I want you to have a good time while I'm gone; be a gold digger with all the boys and see and do things that you missed while going with me. But don't forget me and look forward till the time we can be together and be happy like only you and I can. Believe me when I say the happiest moments of my life have been spent with you.

And I'm looking forward to a lot more with you.

With All My Love,

Bob

---.--/ -...-/.-./.-../../-./--./

February 2, 1943

My Darling Frances,

I received another letter from you today, and as usual, it was one of the best. Darling, they mean so much to me. They keep me going from day to day. I'm so glad to hear that you're happy, Darling, and I'm glad that I can make you so. I hope I can make you even more happy. When I come back, I'm going to make you proud of me. Getting your wings takes a long time, and I'm going to be right in there pitching for you and me.

I hope you're having a good time and don't let that Chemistry class get you down. It's tough, but it's good for you. It should help you plan your college curriculum.

With All My Love and More,

Bob

---.--/ -...-/.-./.-../../-./--./

February 23, 1943

My Darling Frances,

I'm sorry that I had to leave in such a hurry as there were a few things I wanted to say that I didn't get to. Maybe it's better that I didn't. I'm not much at doing a whole lot of talking, especially when

I'm out with you. I'm usually so happy that I forget what I want to say. Frances if you find someone you love more than me while I'm gone, please, don't fool me, but let me know, when you are sure. You won't have to worry about me. I love you very much. You may think this sounds funny, but I hope you don't. I'm a little bit older than you. I've been around a lot; I've seen all types of women and associated with them (you can laugh), but I have. Darling, you're tops with me. You are all I want and ever will want, so don't fool me, because it would be awful hard for me to take.

With All My Love,

Bob

---·--/ -···-/·-·/·-··/··/-·/--·/

Tuesday 8:15 P.M. February 23, 1943

My Darling Frances,

Darling, I've made some swell friends since I've been in the Army. One of my friends played on the Ohio State football team last year. He's a swell guy. In fact, all of the boys in the barracks are good fellows. Another one went to a military school by Nashville. He and I are great pals. He was engaged to be married to a girl, and she suddenly died before he could marry her. Another boy came straight off his honeymoon into the army, and he's taking it pretty hard.

Darling, all I have to do is look at your picture and I'm happy again. I'm living for your letters and the Air Force.

With All My Love,

Bob

---.--/ -...-/.-./.-../../-./--./

Wednesday February 25, 1943

My Darling Frances,

I'm in a good mood today. Last night I dreamed I was out with you, and we had the best time. This morning when I woke up, they issued us our dog tags, and I found out from a reliable source that we are leaving soon, so you see, I had every right in the world to be happy.

With All My Love,

Bob

---.--/ -...-/.-./.-../../-./--./

Bob would later recall, "Boot camp was alright. It was interesting. Our drill sergeant was Tony Martin, who was a popular singer and entertainer during that era. We were pretty fortunate. Boot camp was down in Wichita Falls, Texas, during the summer, and it was hot and dusty. We were all young then, and it didn't bother us. In basic training, I was with another fellow from New Albany who I enlisted with, and he got scarlet fever. They put him in the hospital, and he later flew a B-24. So, we were in quarantine until that was over with. By that time, basic training was over, so I missed out on about half of basic training. It didn't bother me, missing basic training."

After basic training, Bob participated in the College Training Program at Kansas State Teachers College [now Emporia State university] in Emporia, Kansas, for a period of two months. This training was the route to becoming a pilot. Bob had longed to be an airplane pilot since he was a boy riding his bike to Bowman Field to watch the planes take off and land. Now he was finally on his way to fulfilling his dream. Even so, he desperately missed Frances. Their romance had already been interrupted several times, and now they were separated again.

Overall, though, Bob enjoyed the training phase of his military experience. He made new friends and looked forward to becoming a pilot.

---.--/ -...-/.-./.-../../-./--./

March 1, 1943

My Darling Frances,

I'm in Kansas, as I guess you already know. This is the first chance I've had to write you since I got here. It sure is a swell place, and I like it fine. Studies start tomorrow, and I'll probably have less time to write you, but I'll write you every day even though the letters might be short. I'm going to study hard and live for the day I see you again. There is nothing more in the world that I want right now then to have you in my arms.

With All My Love,

Bob

---.--/ -...-/.-./.-../../-./--./

March 5, 1942

My Darling Frances,

Darling, I have everything before me, and all I want you to do is hope and pray that I make good. Maybe with a little luck and common sense I'll make good. Then you can really be proud of me. Right now, I'm only doing what any true American should do. Darling, I'm proud to wear this uniform, and I'm even more thankful I have you backing me every bit of the way. Darling, I've always loved you with all my heart.

With Every Bit of My Love,

Bob

---·--/ -···-/·-·/·-··/··/-·/--·/

March 9, 1943

My Darling Frances,

Right now, I take Geography, History, English, Math, First Aid, and Physical Education. Doesn't exactly sound like a course that a future pilot would take, but that's the way it is. I hope I don't have to spend too much time here at this college. The sooner I get my wings the better I'll like it. Looks like all the boys back home are either in the army or going to be.

As soon as the war is over, Darling, we'll be able to make plans and do whatever we please. I'm going to call home Sunday afternoon. If you think you could go over home then, so I could talk to you and mother on the same call. I don't know if calling home is going to help me or harm me, but I'm going to do it anyway.

With All My Love and More,

Bob

---·--/ -···-/·-·/·-··/··/-·/--·/

Monday March 13, 1943

My Darling Frances,

Well, I've talked to you, and it doesn't hardly seem possible that I did. I was so happy to get to talk to you that I didn't say anything I wanted to, because I was almost speechless. It sure does a soldier good to talk to his mother and girl for the first time in a long time.

I really am quite proud of myself in making the top 100 out of 500 men who are supposed to be the cream of the crop. It lets you still have a chance, and that there are a few people in this world dumber than you are.

With All My Love,

Bob

---·--/ -···-/·-·/·-··/··/-·/--·/

Saturday March 15, 1943

My Darling Frances,

I received the picture in yesterday afternoon's mail and, Darling, I'll always keep it with me wherever I go. If everything goes right, I will get my wings in 9 months from April 1st.

Darling, you wanted to know in one of your letters if we could keep on planning. We've got to. We can't stop planning, that's the only thing we have left as long as we are apart, and we can't lose that. All I have to do is look at your picture, and I get damn homesick for you. If I could just see you for a few minutes, it would mean so much to me. Just one good kiss from you and I'd be floating on air again.

With All My Love for You,

Bob

---·--/ -···-/·-·/·-··/··/-·/--·/

March 16, 1943

My Darling Frances,

I received the birthday cake today, and it really hit the spot. It reminded me of the many times I crashed your mother's Saturday night card game to get a piece of her homemade cakes.

We've got a long wait ahead of us, but I believe we can make it. When the time does come, it will be the happiest day of my life. I only hope, Darling, that you will wait for me. I don't think it will hurt you, because if anything does happen to me, you'll still be young and have all the opportunities in the world.

I do hope you have a good time back home while I'm gone, Darling. Just because I'm not there is no reason why you shouldn't have a good time. Just remember that I love you, and I'll be back some day to prove it. And maybe I'll be worthy of loving you. I only hope so, Darling.

All My Love for You, Darling,

Bob

---.--/ -...-/.-./.-../../-./--./

Saturday March 21, 1943

My Darling Frances,

If you think I haven't been marching since I've been in the army, listen to this. I've already worn one pair of G.I. shoes out.

Darling, the letter I got from you today was the sweetest yet. When you tell me you love me and always will, it does something to me which is nothing short of a miracle. It makes me feel so good to know that I've got everything to look forward to. Today I am 21, and I don't feel a bit older, maybe a little more experienced. I only wish I were back home so I could celebrate it with you. I'm afraid I'm not going to do much celebrating today. Sunday is my worst day. I'm always down in the dumps on Sundays, and today is no exception. I guess it's because I have so much time to think of you on Sundays.

All My Love for You,

Bob

---.--/ -...-/.-./.-../../-./--./

March 24, 1943

My Darling Frances,

I'm sorry that this letter is late, but it couldn't be helped. I've been very busy this week. I've had two tests, one in medical aid and one in mathematics. I made a 100 on the math test and an A on the medical aid test. I've, also, been organizing a squadron basketball team. So, you see, I've been damn busy, but I should have found time to write to you. Don't feel bad if you don't get a letter from me every day. I'll never miss over a day writing to you.

Darling, your letters have really been sweet, and how I love to get them. I hope you're having a good time back home. I want you to have a good time more than anything else. You just keep dreaming and thinking of me, and I'll be more than satisfied.

All My Love for You, Darling,

Bob

---.--/ -...-/.-./.-../../-./--./

March 28, 1943

My Darling Frances,

We get paid this Wednesday, and I have about $70 coming to me. I'm going to send half of it home and the rest has to last me until the first of May. Darling, if I pass this physical at the next place, I think I'll be set for the rest of the way. In the meantime, I just hope and pray that I make it. Darling, I sure agree with you. Love is the most important thing in life, and that makes you the most important thing to me. To be in love with you is really wonderful, and you don't appreciate it to the fullest extent till you've been apart like we have.

With All My Love,

Bob

---.--/ -...-/.-./.-../../-./--./

April 11, 1943

My Darling Frances,

I was up flying five times and really did swell according to my instructor. I flew that airplane just as though I'd been flying all my life. Gee, it sure is great to be able to cruise around up there above this crazy old life. I sure hope I pass the next physical. If I don't, I'll really be heart-broken.

All My Love,

Bob

---·--/ -···-/·-·/·-··/··/-·/--·/

April 19, 1943

My Darling Frances,

If I pass the physical everything will be O.K. I'll, also, be classified as a Pilot, Navigator, or Bombardier. Darling, if I don't pass that physical, I'm going to be really down on the world. But there is nothing I can do about it. I either pass or I don't. I'm afraid if I don't pass it, I'll be a very poor soldier.

All My Love for You, Darling,

Bob

---·--/ -···-/·-·/·-··/··/-·/--·/

April 25, 1942

My Darling Frances,

I wish I was back home with you. You'd be all dressed up as pretty as ever, and I'd probably be dressed sloppy as hell, but I'd sure be happy. We could take a walk or maybe a ride this afternoon. We'd talk about nothing but ourselves and have a swell time doing it. Tonight, I could take you in my arms and be in heaven. Darling, every time I think about you, I get the funniest feeling deep down inside me, and it makes me feel good. It couldn't be anything but love. Darling, I love you so very much, and I never want to lose you.

That's all I live for, to get letters from you.

All my Love for You,

Bob

---·--/ -···-/·-·/·-··/··/-·/--·/

April 28, 1943

My Darling Frances,

I had my eye recheck on my physical today. I found out from that recheck that I can't fly for Uncle Sam. Darling, I guess you know how I feel about not being able to make a pilot. Next to you I loved flying best. But if I can't actually fly one, I want to be one of the crew. If I do get ground duty only, I'm still going to try like hell to make a good soldier. I know what I do won't be much, but it will be my best.

All My Love for You,

Bob

---·--/ -···-/·-·/·-··/··/-·/--·/

May 2, 1943

My Darling Frances,

When I didn't pass my physical test, I'm eligible for ground duty only. I suppose you know what that did to me. I haven't been the same since it happened. At first, I was mad, and then I felt sick as hell, and then I felt like crying my fool head off. Boy, was that ever a blow to me. I feel like I've been hit over the head with the world. Darling, I guess you think I'm a sentimental fool, but flying meant so damn much to me.

Today I had my interview before a board of officers for the Army Special Training program, and I have made it O.K. They are going to send me to Radio School.

All My Love and Lots of Kisses,

Bob

———·——/ —···—/·—·/·—··/··/—·/——·/

Although the Army Air Force had sent Bob to the San Antonio, Texas, Classification Center for additional pilot training, unfortunately, a physical there deemed him ineligible to be a pilot due to an alleged eye deficiency. The Army Air Force routinely dismissed cadets when there was a shortage of gunners, engineers, and radio operators for their heavy bombers. This policy resulted in Bob being trained and assigned as a radio operator. The irony was that radio operators were required to see up close to take and send messages in code. The Army Air Force did not provide Bob with glasses.

Many years later Bob met up with a friend who served with him, Roger Armstrong. Like Bob, Armstrong had also washed out of pilot cadet school and then sent to radio school. Writing about his experiences in the war as a radio operator in his book *USA The Hard Way*, Armstrong explains, "A few years ago, I discussed my cadet experiences with General Curtis E. LeMay, retired Chief of Staff of the United States Air Force. He told me that complete classes of cadets were 'washed out' during this period because air crews were needed in the 8th Air Force due to heavy losses in combat over Germany...I began seeing fellows who had been in my cadet class and found they were also reclassified due to the medical exam at San Antonio. So, it was an arbitrary decision in that the cadet classes were full for flying, navigation, and bombardiers. The cadets were needed for flight engineers, radio operators, and armorers."

---·--/ -···-/·-·/·-··/··/-·/--·/

May 19, 1943

My Darling Frances,

Last night I went to a U.S.O. show. It was an all-star Negro band. It had a sax man from Count Basie, a sax man from Earl Hines, another one by the name of Fletcher Henderson, who was Benny Goodman's arranger, Les Brown's arranger, Christopher Columbus on the drums, and one of his trombone men, and one of Duke Ellington's men on the bass fiddle. They were solid.

I want to make something of myself before we get married. Darling, I hope to be able to give you a secure and happy living. I love you with all my heart, and I don't think anything can stop our love for each other, not even a war. Darling, when we get married, I want to have a home of our own where we can have children and give them every opportunity possible.

I'll be home someday, Darling, and what a day it will be.

All My Love and Lots More,

Bob

---·--/ -···-/·-·/·-··/··/-·/--·/

June 6, 1943,

My Darling Frances,

I dreamed I was home last night, and you came running to me, and I kissed you like I've never kissed you before, and we had the best time.

I think this experience is changing me a lot, Darling, and I don't think it's for the good. It's making me hard and practical, and I don't want to be that way too much. It has made me appreciate religion a lot more than I did. I really get a lot more out of church then I used to.

All My Love for You,

Bob

---·--/ -···-/·-/·-··/··/-·/--·/

June 9, 1943

My Darling Frances,

I go on guard duty Monday, and I'm hoping and praying that I get on shipping before then, because that guard duty is one hell of a job. You're on guard for 2 hours and off for 4 hours for a period of 24 hours, and you stay in the guardhouse till your hitch is over. You walk your duty with full dress uniform including leggings, gas mask, and helmet with a 9 lb. rifle. It's quite a load. Yes, you also, wear a cartridge belt. So much for the Army.

I got a letter from you today, and I feel like a new man. I hope you like your job, and I'm glad you got one. You said you were going to send me a picture of you in your graduation gown. I hope I don't have to wait too long.

With All My Love for You, Beautiful,

Bob

Squadron A, 84th College training detachment (Aircrew). Kansas State Teachers College, Emporia, KS. April 17th, 1943.

Bob Oakes pictured front row, 4th from the left.

Chapter Six

Eighteen Words Per Minute

In the summer of 1943, Bob was next sent to radio school in Sioux Falls, South Dakota, where radio operators were required to process Morse code at least eighteen words per minute. Bob recalled, "They'd give it to you hours at a time. A couple of guys just got up and threw their helmets across the room and walked out. It wasn't hard for me to learn the code."

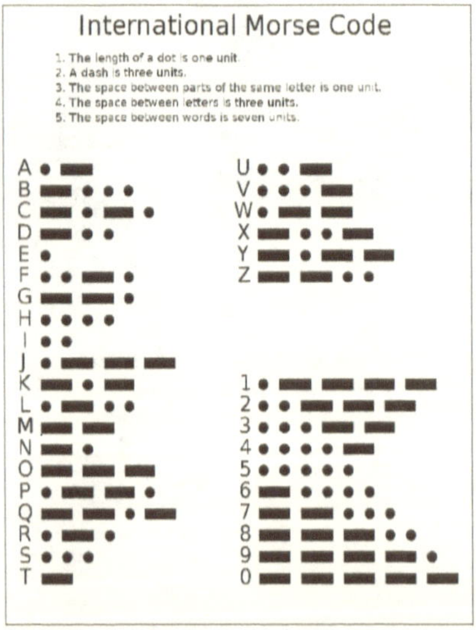

Bob's skill with Morse code was one he never forgot. When he was in his 90s and giving a school presentation, he quickly tapped out some of the students' names on a telegraph key to the amazement of the audience. Even though his dreams to become a pilot were dashed, the training to become a radio operator was a great fit for Bob. Many years later when asked about not becoming a pilot, Bob admitted that he was glad he did not become a pilot because of the extra pressure and responsibilities they endured.

−−−·−−/ −···−/·−·/·−··/··/−·/−−·/

June 19, 1943

My Darling Frances,

Sioux Falls has a population of about 50,000. and it's the largest city in either of the Dakotas. When school starts, I'll go 6 days a week and will go from 6 P.M. to 2 A.M. It's just like working the swing shift for Dupont.

Honey, would you take a ring from me, when I save up enough money to buy you one? Boy, but that was awful. Darling, if you think we should wait awhile, or you don't want it just say so, I won't feel hurt or be mad at you.

All My Love for You,

Bob

−−−·−−/ −···−/·−·/·−··/··/−·/−−·/

July 5, 1943

My Darling Frances,

Yesterday, I celebrated the Fourth of July by going to school and parading around the camp for the benefit of the Commanding Officer. That's a far cry from the way I spent the last Fourth of July. If I remember correctly last Fourth of July we went with Scotty and Bax up to Baxter's cottage and spent the day and went to the show that night. We had one hell of a good time, and I even kissed you a couple of times.

I found out today that I made the honor roll for the first 3 weeks with a 92 average in radio mechanics. I believe I've missed you more this week than I have since I've been in the army. I haven't been able to get you off my mind this week. I thought about you in Theory and instead of copying code like I should, I sat there and thought of you.

All My Love for You, Darling,

Bob

---·--/ -···-/·-·/·-··/··/-·/--·/

July 28, 1943

My Darling Frances,

Believe it or not, Darling, I'm a track man. I ran the 100-yard dash in the track meet today and won the event, which ain't too slow for the first time I ever ran it. Darling, I wouldn't tell you not to go to IU [Indiana University] or to go. It will cost your dad a nice little sum, but at the same time you'll have lots of fun, and it would be good for you.

All My Love for You,

Bob

---·--/ -···-/·-·/·-··/··/-·/--·/

July 31, 1943

My Darling Frances,

I've had a 95 average in Radio Mechanics for the last week, and I think I'll be able to keep that average the next time I'm tested. I'm still on 12 words a minute though, but I'll get off 12 eventually.

All My Love for You, Darling,

Bob

---·--/ -···-/·-·/·-··/··/-·/--·/

August 25, 1943

My Darling Frances,

Well Darling, you wanted to know what I was doing, so I'll tell you. I'm still taking code, and I'm working on 16 words a minute, I don't know when I'll ever make it. They have changed the rules, and now you have to copy 18 words a minute before you graduate. I don't know when I'll ever pass 18, but I guess I'll make it someday. At 18 words a minute that code is really breezing by. You have to copy automatically on 14 words a minute. You hear a continuous noise and your pencil just breezes across the paper. In Radio Mechanics I'm studying a command set that the pilots use for inter plane communications and communications with their base. I tune them and trouble shoot them and then take voltage and resistance measurements on them.

Your Loving Husband to Be,

Bob

---·--/ -···-/·-·/·-··/··/-·/--·/

August 27, 1943

My Darling Frances,

A week from Sunday we change shifts. The shift I'll be going on is one hell of a shift. We start to school at 1:00 A.M. in the morning and finish school at 9:40 A.M., take P.T. from 10:00 A.M. to 12:00

A.M. and that finishes the day. Isn't that one hell of a way for a man to live?

Darling, the more I think about it the more foolish I think you are. I don't know why you love me so much or why you ever think of marrying me. I have no future whatsoever. I don't know what I'll do or how I'll make a living after this war is over. You'll have a better education than I have. You are and will be so much better than I am that it won't be funny. It will be a hard life, Darling. I probably won't be able to give you near the things you should have or want. All I can do is promise you that I'll make you happy. I'll love you with all my heart.

All My Love for You, Darling and a Great Big Kiss,

Bob

---·--/ -···-/·-·/·-··/··/-·/--·/

September 8, 1943

My Darling Frances,

I sure am proud of you now that you are a Kappa Alpha Theta pledge. You'll be right in the swing of things at I.U. being a Theta. Now that you're in the elite don't forget to write me. Do you know, Darling, that 8 months is a long time to be away from you? These 8 months have only made me love you more than ever, and made me realize that I can't live without you.

I'm working on 18 words a minute.

Every Bit of My Love for You, Darling,

Bob

---·--/ -···-/·-·/·-··/··/-·/--·/

September 22, 1943

My Darling Frances,

I've been sewing on PFC [Private First Class] stripes all week. You should have seen me. I had everyone in the barracks in an uproar. I spent half an hour sewing on an emblem. I really took great pains, and it was a real good job. As I proudly gloated over it, I discovered I had sewn it on the right sleeve instead of the left sleeve. You can imagine what I said. The boys in the barracks got a great kick out of my sewing experience at my expense.

All My Love to You, Darling,

Bob

---·--/ -···-/·-·/·-··/··/-·/--·/

September 30, 1943

My Darling Frances,

I suppose IU is missing a lot of the college color it had before the war, but you'll like it a lot better after you've been there a month or two. I've just been thinking, we sure have written a lot of letters to each other. I wrote to you first when I was at Purdue, and I've been writing to you off and on ever since. I just wonder how many letters we have written to each other.

Darling, I don't know if I told you, or if it will even interest you, but I now have credit for 18 words of code per minute, and that's what it takes to graduate.

All My Love for You,

Bob

---.--/ -...-/.-./.-../../-./--./

October 19, 1943

My Darling Frances,

How's my little college girl, sweet and lovely? How would you like to be starting out on a heavy date with me right now? Wouldn't that be strictly on the beam? Where would we go first?

I mailed your graduation present, a bracelet, yesterday. You'll probably get it before you get this letter. In exactly three weeks from today, if nothing happens, I'll graduate from this school as a Radio Operator and Mechanic. One week after I graduate, I should ship and I'll be glad when that time comes.

All My Love and More,

Bob

---.--/ -...-/.-./.-../../-./--./

October 29, 1943

My Darling Frances,

I sure am happy to graduate on time. More than 50% of the class washed back [had to retake the class] including my best friend, but that's the army. Next week I'll be flying all the time, but not at the stick. Instead, I'll be twisting knobs and keeping in touch with the ground, and it'll be a medium bomber B-26 Martin Marauder and it's my favorite ship, "hot as hell though." It lands around 130 miles per hour. This radio operator ain't a bad deal. After I finish gunnery, I'll be on flying pay with a sergeant's rating and that kind of money ain't hay.

All My Love, Darling,

Bob

---·--/ -···-/·-·/·-··/··/-·/--·/

November 10, 1943,

My Darling Frances,

After graduation in the morning, the gang (including me) went to town and celebrated our graduation by getting really well plastered. After 20 weeks of this radio school, I felt well justified in my actions. I'm going to gunnery school from here which lasts 6 weeks. If I get through OK I will be made a sergeant and will also get either a furlough or a 10 day delay in route which will be welcomed by "Yours Truly" whole heartedly. Darling, it's going to be heaven when that happens. We know that for sure, and besides, I'll be wearing sergeant stripes and silver wings by then. At least I'll have something to show for a year's service in the Army.

With All My Love and More,

Bob

---·--/ -···-/·-·/·-··/··/-·/--·/

Besides knowing Morse code, radio operators also had to be able to maintain the radio equipment. In a room, students were given radio sets, all of which had some sort of malfunction. Each student was assigned a set and tasked with finding the problem. Bob recalled one trainee who slaved over his set and never could find the problem, finally telling the instructor at the end of the session that he couldn't find the issue. The instructor told him to try plugging it in.

After six months of training, Bob graduated and was shipped to gunnery school in Yuma, Arizona. He finished gunnery school second in gunnery accuracy. Hunting squirrels in the woods of southern Indiana with his uncles had paid off.

"Even as a radio operator, I was issued a .50 caliber machine gun," Bob said. "We had thirteen .50 caliber machine guns on the B-17, each of which could shoot a thousand feet. When all of them were going off it sure was noisy."

---·--/ -···-/·-·/·-··/··/-·/--·/

November 23, 1943

My Darling Frances,

Arrived here in Yuma, Arizona late yesterday afternoon after a long and tiresome train ride. This field is in a desert, near the edge. The desert is over 100 miles long and extends through California to the coast. We're living in tents which isn't as bad as it sounds, as they have wooden floors and wooden sides 5' tall. They are very easy to keep clean. It's really warm through the day time, warm enough to run around without a shirt on, but at night you use every blanket you can find to keep warm. I will graduate from this gunnery school around January 10th, then the delay in route, "oh happy day." I think this gunnery school is going to be very good and interesting. They have a bunch of the latest models of the B-17s down here to train us in, and they are a sweet ship if I ever saw one.

That phone call I made to you boosted my morale 100%, and I don't mean maybe. Just hearing you talk does more to me than you'll ever know, Darling. Just think, in less than a month and a half I'll be able to take you in my arms and tell you how much I really love you, as if you didn't already know.

All My Love for You, Darling,

Bob

---·--/ -···-/·-·/·-··/··/-·/--·/

November 27, 1943

My Darling Frances,

Just think, I'll be home for 10 whole days and nights. It's hard to believe. I have 6 more weeks of gunnery, and then I'll be home.

They have a lot of B-17's to train us in down here. Week after next, we fly to Santa Anita, California in B-17's. I wish I could make it home for Christmas, but it can't be done, and I guess I'm lucky to get home at all. I sure wish I could be with you tonight. For some reason I miss you something terrible tonight. You would think that being away from you as long as I have, I'd get over missing you to a certain extent, but I don't. I know why. It's because I love you so very, very much and will forever.

Every Bit of My Love for You, Honey,

Bob

---·--/ -···-/·-·/·-··/··/-·/--·/

December 5, 1943

My Darling Frances,

Was up in a B-17 yesterday for about 2 hours, and they had pursuit ships diving at us at all times. We had to call their positions out over the interphones and point our guns at them like we would in actual combat. It was lots of fun.

All My Love for You,

Bob

---·--/ -···-/·-·/·-··/··/-·/--·/

December 9, 1943

My Darling Frances,

Darling, about the ring, I'm sure my parents will not object as they like you very much, and I know they want me to be happy. I hope your mother doesn't object too much, because more than anything in the world I want to give you a ring. I don't know why your mother doesn't like me or approve of me. Maybe it's because she doesn't think I'm good enough. That might be right, but I can't help it if I love you as much as I do. I do hope she changes her mind about the whole thing as it would make it much better.

All My Love to You, Darling,

Bob

---·--/ -···-/·-·/·-··/··/-·/--·/

December 15, 1943

My Darling Frances,

Did you listen to Bob Hope last night? He broadcast from the field and we got to see the broadcast and a show afterwards. He was really good. Next Thursday we get all of our flying clothes and equipment issued to us. We sure get a lot of stuff. We have summer and winter flying suits, oxygen mask, 2 flight jackets (winter and summer), parachute, and a lot of other stuff.

I'll take care of your mother. I'll write her the sweetest letter I know how.

All My Love for You, Sweet,

Bob

---·--/ -···-/·-·/·-··/··/-·/--·/

December 20, 1943

My Darling Frances,

We graduate January 10, and allowing 3 days for traveling, I'll be home sometime between January 13-16. Darling, when I do get in the fight, you'll know that I'm fighting for you and when it's for you, I can't lose.

I can hardly wait to see you, the way you smile at me, and to hear you talk, and more than anything, to dance with you again and to have that beautiful hair tickle me in the face.

Those blue eyes of yours always did get me, and the way you kissed me, and just think all of those things will happen to me again in a very short time. Just think, Darling, it's about a year since I last saw you, and that's a long time to be away from one you love so much.

All of My Love for You, Darling,

Bob

---·--/ -···-/·-·/·-··/··/-·/--·/

January 2, 1944

My Darling Frances,

I like the idea fine about you meeting me at the train station and then surprising the folks. In fact, it's a damn good idea. Darling, they're playing "Stardust" over the radio and all I have to do is think about you and listen to the music and I'm out of this world.

With All My Love and More,

Bob

---·--/ -···-/·-·/·-··/··/-·/--·/

During his ten-day leave in January 1944, Bob purchased an engagement ring for Frances. He had mustered up enough money with help from his brother, Marvin, to buy a small diamond ring. Frances' father took Bob to a jeweler friend for help in choosing the right one. Frances took the week off from her classes at Indiana University, and they were engaged! Bob's ten-day leave went by too quickly, and they parted again.

---·--/ -···-/·-·/·-··/··/-·/--·/

January 25, 1944

My Darling Frances,

Darling, I guess you know I'm the happiest guy living right now. That I've lost my grip, if I ever had one, and that I'm about to go crazy being away from you. On the way home from Bloomington [Indiana University] I felt awful. I just didn't care what happened. All I could think about was that I was going away from you, and there was nothing I could do about it. Darling, the night of the dance you were more beautiful and gorgeous than ever. I'm convinced your mother is happy about our engagement, and that relieves my mind of a big load. When I told her goodbye, she put her arms around me and kissed me on the cheek. She told me to take care of myself, and I think she meant it with all her heart. If everything turns out good, and I come through this war O.K. nothing will stop our happiness then.

All My Love for You, Darling,

Bob

---·--/ -···-/·-·/·-··/··/-·/--·/

In his letters to Frances, Bob captured his sense of apprehension about the war's potential effect on their relationship. They were caught in a terrible situation that they had very little control over. They were separated and fate would determine their future.

---·--/ -···-/·-·/·-··/··/-·/--·/

January 30, 1944

My Darling Frances,

You remember what I kept telling everybody what the Air Force had in store for Germany? Well, I just heard over the radio that 6,000 of our planes had bombed Germany. That's a lot of planes. That's 3 times as many planes as we had in the whole Air Force when the war started.

All My Love for You, Sweet,

Bob

---·--/ -···-/·-·/·-··/··/-·/--·/

February 3, 1944

My Darling Frances,

Someone is singing "Night and Day" on the radio and It's giving me that wonderful feeling. The words express my thoughts perfectly. When I get to thinking about you so much, I can't stand it. I get your picture out and just sit and stare at it, and relive that wonderful weekend we had.

Darling, I agree with you that as for us getting married is concerned, the only sensible thing we can do is wait till the war is over, and I can come back to you for good. I know that God must be on our side and will make it possible for us to enjoy our happiness to the fullest extent. I pray every night that he will take care of us.

All My Love to You, Darling, and More,

Bob

---·--/ -···-/·-·/·-··/··/-·/--·/

March 22, 1944

My Darling Frances,

Yesterday was my 22nd birthday, and I went to town to celebrate with a few of the boys and the help of a few drinks.

Ours is a wonderful love, Darling, and we should be very thankful for it. A love that can make people as happy as us when we're together is really something to talk about and fight to live for.

I Love You Forever and Ever, Darling,

Bob

---·--/ -···-/·-·/·-··/··/-·/--·/

April 2, 1944

My Darling Frances,

I went to church tonight and took communion. It was really a nice service, and I got a lot of benefit out of it. Give me one of those wonderful kisses of yours in my dreams tonight, and I'll be a happy man.

Love for You Forever,

Bob

Chapter Seven

The Battle of the Skies

During his military service, Bob experienced several lucky events that were critical to his survival during the war. The first lucky break was that his stateside training lasted one year, ten months, and nine days. The significance of this was that critical lessons about air warfare were learned in combat during his training period. These insights and changes were incorporated into Army Air Force operations and greatly improved Bob's chances of coming home safely.

I Want You WWII Army poster.

The Development of Air Warfare

Starting in World War I, airplanes became a tactical force as part of war. In WWII, from 1939 until 1944, Germany was decidedly in control of the skies over Europe. The world witnessed the integral part that air warfare played in Germany's lightning conquest of most of Europe.

Essentially, the German Blitzkrieg was a strategy that combined attacks by German soldiers and Panzer tank divisions with the German Luftwaffe, or air force, which included both fighter and bomber planes. The Blitzkrieg annihilated the defenses of any country that stood in its way. Quickly, the Nazis conquered Poland, France, Belgium, and any other European country that they wanted to conquer.

Germany also led the way in strategic air warfare with its attacks against England, the last holdout against the Third Reich's mighty war machine. The British Royal Air Force sent its vastly outnumbered air crews to tackle the German bombers and fighters in the Battle of Britain, which lasted from July 10, 1940, until October 31, 1940. The British fighter planes held their own against the German Messerschmitt airplane fighters and shot down enough German bombers to make it too costly for Germany to continue their plans to invade England.

As British Prime Minister Winston Churchill so famously said, referring to the extraordinary efforts of the Royal Air Force and the Polish No. 303 Squadron Royal Air Force in the Battle of Britain, "Never in the field of human conflict was so much owed by so many to so few."

After failing to gain air superiority over Great Britain, Hitler turned his attention to the conquest of Russia and postponed the invasion of England. Some believe this was Hitler's greatest mistake when he divided German forces between two military fronts, the Soviet Union and England, while also ignoring the imminent threat of the United States.

Upon entering WWII, the relatively new United States Army Air Force was striving to become a part of the Allies' air threat. This involved protecting ground forces, bombing enemy forces and enemy-held combat areas, and taking out supply lines and transportation.

What could this new air war strategy produce? Air combat engaged in by airplane fighters high in the skies had been important in gaining air superiority as shown by the British fighters in the Battle of Britain. But what part would heavy bomber planes serve?

Several key questions had to be worked out. The most important was how to get maximum use out of the bombers to destroy the enemy. This was a trial-and-error process that was paid for with high casualty numbers and a huge loss of airplanes. It was a bloody initiation.

In *Bombers of WWII,* Jeffrey Ethell writes, "Of all the combat jobs in the American services during WWII, from infantrymen to submariner, no job was more dangerous statistically, than that of a man in a bomber airplane over Germany. The Eighth and Fifteenth Air Forces flying over Germany took a higher percentage of losses than any other American fighting force, from foxhole to destroyer deck."

Bob was about to enter the fray, taking his place among the other bomber boys in WWII's most dangerous job, flying deep into enemy territory.

Preparing for D-Day from the Skies

In early January 1943, British Prime Minister Winston Churchill, President Franklin Roosevelt, and the top military chiefs from both countries met in Casablanca, Morocco, to hammer out the next strategies and priorities of the war. It was at Casablanca that the decision was made that the Allies would plan for a combined bombing offensive against Germany. The Casablanca Directive set out the priorities for the campaign. The targets for the Allied forces would be the destruction and obstruction of Germany's ability to wage war.This would include bombing German submarine construction, aircraft production, transportation systems, and petroleum facilities. The specific bombing targets and the order of their importance changed as the war progressed, but the key idea of destroying Germany's ability to wage war never altered.

Early on, the Allies knew that air superiority over the landing beaches for the big invasion in France, D-Day, June 6, 1944, had to be won. Soldiers clawing for footholds on the beaches of Normandy would be destroyed if enemy airplanes were machine gunning and bombing the landing sites from above. The German Luftwaffe had to be dealt a crippling blow.

How were heavy bombers used in the war preparing for D-Day? Crippling the enemy's ability to wage war by destroying or disrupting its manufacturing and transportation capabilities became the priority. Heavy bombers could drop bombs deep inside enemy territory. A major two-hit strategy was developed for August 17, 1943. The German Messerschmitt fighter airplane factory at Regensburg, Germany, would be hit along with an attack on the ball-bearing plant at Schweinfurt, Germany.

In *Flying Fortress* by Edward Jablonski, he quotes General Ira C. Eaker, Commander of the Eighth Army Air Force as saying, "It was one of the great air battles of the pre-invasion effort to reduce the Luftwaffe to impotence, so that a seaborne land invasion of Europe could be made without prohibitive casualties. Schweinfurt-Regensburg was a dramatic symbol of the strategic air operations, which made it impossible for that force to be of any consequence against the Allied landings in France on June 6, 1944. The gallant sacrifices of the of the 8th Air Force bomber crews saved thousands of lives of Allied sailors and soldiers crossing the beaches on D-Day." More than 60 bombers and 600 crewmen were lost in this one Allied offensive.

Along with the crippling of the German airplane industry before D-Day, the Allies developed the Transportation Plan. This called for the bombers to cripple the French railway system and destroy French bridges. Eisenhower insisted that German military mobility be severely hampered in France to ensure that the Nazis would have difficulty in counter-attacking the Allied landing on D-Day and in the days after the first assault on German defenses.In *The Victors*, Stephen Ambrose writes, "The bombers went to work, dropping seventy-six thousand tons of bombs on rail centers, bridges, and open lines."

Another effect of the Allies' bombing attacks on Germany's war manufacturing and on German cities was that the number of fighter planes needed to protect Germany had to be increased. This reduced the number of the Luftwaffe fighter planes fighting in other parts of Europe and on the Russian front. As a result, Allied troops fighting through western Europe had fewer enemy planes attacking them. The Luftwaffe was on the defensive.

Thanks to the Allies' air war, on D-Day the only planes in the sky over Normandy were friendly aircraft. This was achieved at a high price by American and British airmen. Don Miller writes in *Masters of the Air* that, "Seventy-seven percent of the Americans who flew against the Reich before D-Day would wind up casualties."

Unfortunately, the Germans were quick to rebuild their bombed-out factories using forced labor. Soon, they were back to peak production of fighter airplanes. The German economy was more resilient than the Allies had thought, and the German aircraft industry continued to grow through 1943 and 1944. The problem for Germany was pilots. It took time and fuel to train air crews, and Germany was increasingly low on both commodities. New German pilots were insufficiently trained to engage with well-trained American and British fighter pilots. The advantage in the skies, bought with great air crew casualties and loss of planes, gradually turned to the Allies' favor.

Fighting on two fronts at the same time combined with the long-range bombing eventually made an impact on Germany's war machine. However, even with a reduced threat from Luftwaffe a year after the concentrated efforts to destroy the enemy's fighter planes, flying into enemy territory continued to be very costly for the American and British bomber crews. The Germans strengthened their defense of key targets, and the skies over German-held territories remained deadly until the end of the war.

The B-17G and Long-Range Bombing

On August 16, 1943, the B-17 bomber airplanes were upgraded to the B-17G bomber airplane model. Thankfully, Bob was assigned to a B-17G model. The B-17G model had a longer range, more gunfire, and many refinements in radar and bombing equipment as compared to earlier models. Added to these improvements, Allied fighter planes were now capable of flying escort for the bombers all the way to and from the targets deep in enemy territories. These American fighter planes were free to engage in more aerial fights with the German Luftwaffe fighters.

Flying techniques of long-range bombing missions had been acquired through great sacrifices. These techniques were successfully integrated into the successive methods of heavy bombing. The result? Allied bombing was starting to make a difference in Germany's ability to wage war.

The British and American Air Forces were bound by a common goal to destroy the enemy with long-range bombing, but their methodology evolved into two different approaches. The British held on to night bombings. Night bombings were safer for the bombers and their crews, but they were less accurate. This factor did not deter the Royal Air Force from what was called "carpet bombing" of large-area targets at night. The Americans bombed during the day. Their goal was to hit the enemy targets precisely and with as few civilian casualties as possible.

Of course, being completely accurate was impossible. There would be mistakes and stray bombs and a multitude of other factors that could deter bombs from hitting their intended targets with great precision. Still, the accuracy of the Fifteenth Air Force bombing had risen to 50 percent in August 1944 from eighteen percent in April 1944. With the British bombing at night and the Americans during the day, the two forces working together chipped away at Germany's ability to fight.

Bob in his Air Force flying gear.

Long-range bombing needed to be figured out as well as what targets to hit in order to gain the best results from limited resources of trained crews, planes, fuel, and ground support. Essential elements in Germany's war machine were top priority targets. These included fuel refineries, ball bearing factories, munitions factories, and manufacturing centers for airplanes, tanks, and armaments. Disrupting transportation centers came next. At first, heavy bombers were also used to attack submarine pens, but this proved to be a waste of that resource.

The Fighter Escorts

The B-17 bomber plane was so well armed with machine guns that high command initially thought that the plane could fly without fighter escort to and from the bombing targets. This proved to be wrong. When Bob began flying missions in August 1944, the P-51 Mustang fighter planes, nicknamed like other fighter planes, the Little Friends, had been in service escorting bombers since 1943, helping to tip the battle of the skies to the Allies. The P-51 fighter planes flew escort for Bob's bomber group. Another good break for him.

The P-51 was a superb fighter plane, possibly the best in the war, as it had a great climb rate and was faster and more maneuverable than the German fighter planes. It was equipped with six .50-caliber weapons, three in each wing. Perhaps the most notable aspect of the P-51 was that it could escort Allied bombers all the way to their targets deep into Germany.

While doing escort duty, the P-51 fighters engaged the German Luftwaffe fighters who were on the defensive when Bob began flying bombing missions. The Germans were good pilots with good airplanes, but the Mustangs had advantages that they put to use. The word was out to the Americans to engage as many German fighters in combat as possible. The results of the Allied fighters being released to seek out and engage enemy fighters soon took a toll on the German Luftwaffe fighters.

Bob recalled, "Our fighter escorts would sometimes see a train down below, and they loved going after trains. You'd see them dive down right at them. The Germans would have a flat car out in the front with an 88-millimeter gun, but that gun could only aim so low, so when the fighters would fly down on the deck [very close to the ground, 100 feet or lower] they could easily hit that locomotive. From up in the air, you'd see it just blow up. So, the fighters would leave you sometimes when they shouldn't, but generally speaking, we always had good protection. We had escort all the way to the target and all the way back. They broke off just before the actual bombing run, as they were directed to do."

Seven fighter groups were assigned to the Fifteenth Air Force. One of the groups was the 332nd fighter group, the Tuskegee Airmen. The 332nd fighter group was trained at the Tuskeegee Insititue (now Tuskeegee University) in Tuskeegee, Alabama. This African American unit was equipped with the new P-51 Mustang. For easy identification the whole tail section of their planes was painted red, so they were called the Red Tails. Unfortunately, there was an element that did not believe that the African American pilots would be as good in combat as other pilots, but the Tuskegee Airmen more than proved their worth with an impressive war combat record. "The total number of [Tuskegee] escorted bombers shot down [by the Germans] was significantly less than the average number of bombers lost by the six other fighter escort groups of the Fifteenth Air Force." "On the longest fighter-escort mission from Italy to Berlin, three Tuskegee Airmen each shot down a German jet that could fly significantly faster than their own red-tailed P-51 Mustangs."

Bob ranked them the best fighter group his squadron had as escorts, and his squadron was always glad to see the Red Tails flying with them into enemy territory. On several occasions, Bob witnessed a Red Tail fighter destroy an enemy fighter that was attacking his bomber squadron. The Red Tails never forgot their primary purpose as escorts was to protect the B-17 bombers from enemy fighter attacks. They stayed with their bombers and were true escorts all the way into German territory and back home. The heroic service of the Red Tails had a profound and intensely personal impact on Bob.

In November 2009, The National WWII Museum in New Orleans completed their second building which houses the Solomon Victory Theater, the Stage Door Canteen, and the American Sector Restaurant. The museum invited WWII veterans to attend the opening event. Over 300 veterans attended, including Bob. Many celebrities participated in the event that featured Tom Hanks, Tom Brokaw, Mickey Rooney, and other celebrities.

Tuskegee Airmen were among the veterans present. It was an outstanding day with most of the activities occurring outside. The weather was beautiful. Guests found their seats, a military band began to play, and the WWII veterans proudly marched in, led by the Army veterans with their theme song playing. Then Navy, Marines, Coast Guard, and Army Air Force veterans marched in, all accompanied by their theme songs. The veterans were followed by active-duty military. After the official speeches and ceremonies ended, the veterans were treated to a lunch served by the celebrities, the first viewing of the National WWII Museum's 4-D movie, *Beyond All Boundaries*, and given the chance to meet the celebrities.

After the ceremonies, Bob sought out the Tuskegee Airmen. He shook hands and personally thanked every Red Tail airman attending the event for protecting him on his bombing missions. It was an emotional encounter for all involved. The bomber crews and the fighter pilots had never met during their service except in the skies above enemy territory, where they communicated over the radio to each other and had limited visual contact as they flew into combat. The fighter escorts and the heavy bombers had faced death and danger together but separately. Their shared combat experiences had forged a strong, if invisible, bond. During this day of celebration at The National WWII Museum, 65 years later, a grateful bomber crewman was finally able to thank some of the men who had protected him in the air in the summer and fall of 1944.

The National WWII Museum proudly displays a Tuskegee Red Tail P-51 Mustang fighter plane suspended from the ceiling of the Boeing Building Freedom Pavilion alongside a B-17 bomber. The Little Friend is showcased still doing its duty of protecting and escorting the big bomber.

Catching Flak

When Bob began flying missions in 1944, the air superiority had shifted to the Allies' favor, but the number of German defensive flak guns employed against the Allied bombers had increased as Germany desperately defended itself. Flak guns actually posed a bigger threat to the B-17 bombers than enemy fighter planes, as it is estimated that more American planes were shot down by flak than shot down by enemy fighter planes.

The term flak was slang for the German word *Fleigerabwehrkanone*, or anti-aircraft gun. Obviously, the nickname flak was much easier to pronounce. The flak gun used to shoot down Allied bombers was the 88-millimeter. This size flak gun was also used effectively for ground fighting, most notably as an anti-tank weapon. It took from six to ten people to operate. Important German cities and targets were heavily protected with them. Main bomber approach routes were also defended with flak guns. The more essential a target was to the Germans, the more heavily it was protected by flak guns.

When a bomber was close to the target, it was committed to the final run to drop its bombs. At that point, the bomber could not deviate from its flight path. Once the flak gunners on the ground determined the altitude of the bombers and their flight path over the target, they aimed the flak guns accordingly, as the flak shells had a fuse set to explode at the same altitude as the B-17s. This made the bomber planes bullseyes in the sky.

When the flak shell exploded, it created a large puff of black smoke, scattering shrapnel in all directions. At times, the flak would be so thick that it looked like a large black cloud. The flak would rock the aircraft and scatter fragments through the thin aluminum aircraft covering, wounding crew members and damaging the plane. There was nothing the crews could do to defend themselves from flak. They just had to sit there and take it. There was no place to hide, and watching other planes go down from flak damage was a gut-wrenching experience. It was strictly luck that determined the crew's fate during the final miles of the bombing run.

Chapter Eight

The Hour Has Come

After graduating from gunnery school in January 1944, Bob had a ten-day leave, during which time he gave Frances an engagement ring. After that, the Army Air Force sent Bob to Salt Lake City, Utah, where he was assigned to a B-17 bomber crew. Finally, the many months of training were coming to a close. Going into air combat was about to become a reality. There remained only a few stages to complete, then Bob would join the fight.

---·--/ -···-/·-·/·-··/··/-·/--·/

April 5, 1944

My Darling Frances,

I'm first radio operator on a B-17 "Flying Fortress." I've met all the enlisted men on my crew, and they're all swell guys. I haven't met the pilot or copilot as yet. Some of the boys in the crew have, and they say that they're both pretty good "Joes." I'm afraid that I'm not going to get a furlough before I go across. I'll graduate out of here as a Staff Sergeant. That's two grades above my present rating. I'll make $159 a month as long as I'm in the states, and $173 a month overseas. I live for the day that I can be with the sweetest girl that ever lived.

I'll Love You Forever, Sweet,

Bob

---·--/ -···-/·-·/·-··/··/-·/--·/

April 9, 1944

My Darling Frances,

My crew has decided that we'll be back home for Christmas with 25 missions under our belt. Darling, that's not so far off, and I get 30 days furlough when I come back from overseas.

They made us make out a Last Will and Testament and a Power of Attorney, Friday, and told us to send it home. I can just see what kind of effect that will have on Mother. I guess that's a good way of letting her know that I won't be in the states much longer. I hope and pray with all my heart that everything turns out O.K. for us, and I believe with all my heart that it will. I'm going to try my darndest to bring my heart back to you.

All My Love for You, Sweet,

Bob

---·--/ -···-/·-·/·-··/··/-·/--·/

"We were all new on our crew," Bob noted. "Some crews had pilots with some hours of experience flying, but neither our pilot or copilot had any combat flying time. A crew gets to be like family. When you first join up with them you look around and think maybe you don't like this one or that one, but when you get down to it later, you're really close."

The crew was then shipped to Dalhart, Texas, for operational training. The B-17 bombers they trained in were in bad shape. The crew was ordered to fly with the plane's landing gear in the down position because several times the landing gear would not work. The Dalhart Army Air Base, aside from being cold and muddy, was packed with broken-down aircraft. It was a miserable experience for the flight crews.

---·--/ -···-/·-·/·-··/··/-·/--·/

April 11, 1944

My Darling Frances,

From everything they tell us down here we are pretty certain to go to England, which suits me O.K. I heard a red-hot rumor that we are going to be sent to Gulfport, Miss. around the first of May to finish our training. That's where Marvin is. I wish it would come true. I'd get to see Marvin, and it would really be nice to have you come and see me.

I Love You Forever, Darling,

Bob

---·--/ -···-/·-·/·-··/··/-·/--·/

April 17, 1944

My Darling Frances,

I've been flying 6 hours a day and going to ground school for 4 hours a day, so you see, I don't have much time to myself. That Gulfport rumor is turning into a reality. My pilot told me today that a big shot Major told him that we were going to Gulfport around the first of May. Going to Gulfport means a lot to me. It means that I might get a furlough, and I'll get to see Marvin.

I Love You Forever, Darling,

Bob

---·--/ -···-/·-·/·-··/··/-·/--·/

April 21, 1944

My Darling Frances,

I miss you so damn much tonight. I don't know if it's the Texas moon or what it is. It seems as though we've spent more time apart than we have together. This war makes me so mad; just to think that so called civilized people can't think of anything better to do than shoot at one another. It just doesn't make sense. They say we're pretty sure to go to England for combat. If they just send me to Gulfport, and I'll get to see you before I go across, I'll go a contented man.

All My Love for You, Darling,

Bob

---·--/ -···-/·-·/·-··/··/-·/--·/

April 28, 1944

My Darling Frances,

No one can make me mad today. I found out that we're going to Gulfport for sure. It's too good to be true. I can't make myself believe it. I am going to town tonight and celebrate going to Gulfport with a big chicken dinner.

With All My Love, Darling, for You,

Bob

---·--/ -···-/·-·/·-··/··/-·/--·/

After a month, the B-17 crew that Bob was with transferred to Gulfport, Mississippi, for the remainder of operational training. On the way from Dalhart to Gulfport, Bob had an interesting experience. He went to sleep in an Army pullman-type sleeper train car. The next morning, he awoke, and the train was moving in a strange manner, rocking back and forth, without the clickety-clack of the train tracks. He looked out the window, and all he could see was muddy water. The train had been moved onto a ferry boat to cross the Mississippi River in the middle of the night while Bob slept. Once back on land, the train completed its last leg to Gulfport, Mississippi. As soon as Bob got off the train, he saw his brother, Marvin, who was a captain in the Army and ran an officer's club until the war's end.

---·--/ -···-/·-·/·-··/··/-·/--·/

May 5, 1944

My Darling Frances,

Arrived in Gulfport yesterday and Marvin was at the train to get me. He's attached to the same squadron I'm in, so I guess, I'll be seeing a lot of him. We had a long talk last night. They don't have many planes down here right now, and everything seems to be pretty well screwed up. Sometimes I wonder if this army knows which side is up.

All My Love for You, Darling,

Bob

---.--/ -...-/.-./.-../../-./--./

May 9, 1944

My Darling Frances,

Well, I've spent enough time at Gulfport to know what the deal is. The post and town are strictly OK. The 3rd Air Force personnel and the way they are treating us is a horse of another color, but there is nothing I or anyone else can do about it.

You should see Marvin. I mean to tell you, this army has really changed that guy. You should see him operate.

We still don't know if we are going to get a furlough. As soon as I find out what the deal is, we'll try and make some plans. Until then, there is nothing we can do about it.

I flew today for the first time at Gulfport. It was a good flight. We have our brand-new ships. They are really OK. By the way, I had to get up at 3:00 A.M., and that's just a little early even for me.

I don't think it will be so very long before we'll be together again for a short time. Even if it is for only a short time, it will mean everything to me, because I love you so very much. All I want is one of those wonderful kisses of yours.

All My Love Forever, Darling,

Bob

---·--/ -···-/·-·/·-··/··/-·/--·/

May 14, 1944

My Darling Frances,

As far as I can see there is no furlough in view for me. Damn this army anyway. I don't mind going across, but I can't see why in the hell they can't let me go home, and say goodbye to my future wife.

I don't know if I told you or not, but the day before yesterday we flew to Knoxville, Tenn., and yesterday we went to Chattanooga, Tenn., but we didn't land as we never do.

My Love for You, All of It,

Bob

---·--/ -···-/·-·/·-··/··/-·/--·/

Before going into battle, Bob intensely wanted to see Frances. The day was coming quickly when he would be actively using his combat training. The reality that he may not survive was always lurking in the background of their lives. They did not discuss the possibility of his not coming home openly in their letters, but it was always there. He wanted one more chance to hold her in his arms and to speak of their happy future together.

---·--/ -···-/·-·/·-··/··/-·/--·/

May 18, 1944

My Darling Frances,

Darling, you still haunt me all day long, I guess I look as though I'm in a daze most of the time. I think of that wonderful long hair of yours, your beautiful blue eyes, and your kisses. What can you expect? I guess I really am in a daze. But I do know that I love you very, very much and nothing will ever change that no matter what happens. How I wish I could have you in my arms right now and kiss you and tell you how much I really love you, mess your hair up, and lay my head on your shoulder, and dream of the day you'll be my wife.

That's all for now, Darling, see you tonight in my dreams.

All My Love for My Future Wife,

Bob

---.--/ -...-/.-./.-../../-./--./

May 19, 1944

My Darling Frances,

Honey, I'm missing you like all hell tonight, and the only thing I can do to help it, is reminisce about the wonderful times we've had in the past. Like that first kiss we had when I came home on furlough after a year of yearning to hold you in my arms. That was the closest to heaven on earth I ever was. Darling, I want to hold you in my arms tonight, and tell you I love you so very dearly.

All My Love, Darling, for You,

Bob

---·--/ -···-/·-·/·-··/··/-·/--·/

May 28, 1944

My Darling Frances,

Darling, I think the best time for you to come down would be around the 7th of June when my parents come down. Honey, I was pretty close to home the other day. We made a camera mission on the railroad yard at Nashville. I had a good notion to bail out and hitch hike the rest of the way home.

With All My Love and More,

Bob

---·--/ -···-/·-·/·-··/··/-·/--·/

Frances, with Bob's parents, traveled by train to Gulfport to see Bob and his brother, Marvin, before Bob was shipped overseas to combat. Besides enjoying time with their sons and Frances, Bob's parents did some sightseeing. They all took a side trip to New Orleans. While enjoying the French Quarter in New Orleans, Bob and Frances managed to slip away from his parents. The happy couple found their way to The Sazerac Bar in the Roosevelt hotel and enjoyed a drink. Bob and Frances spoke of that magical escape the rest of their lives. It was a short respite from the stress and strain of their situation, a moment alone to shove aside the fears and uncertainty of their future. Too quickly, it was back to reality. Frances was soon back in Indiana, and Bob was preparing for combat. To this day, the descendants of Bob and Frances gather at The Sazerac Bar in The Roosevelt Hotel New Orleans to make their annual toast to Bob and Frances.

---.--/ -...-/.-./.-../../-./--./

June 13, 1944

My Darling Frances,

I can't tell you how much I appreciate your coming down to see me, but, Darling, I think you know how much it meant to me. It meant everything.

Darling, did anyone ever tell you, you are wonderful? Well, I'm telling you right now you are. You're sweet, very understanding, lovable, beautiful, and I love you very much. I'm having a hell of a time getting any sleep since you left. All I do is think about you and how happy we're going to be when this mess is over.

Huffman just put a big bug of some sort in Raught's bed, of course.

All My Love, Darling, for You,

Bob

---.--/ -...-/.-./.-../../-./--./

June 19, 1944

My Darling Frances,

I received your cakes the other day, but I was unable to eat any of them until today. I've been sick for the last couple of days, but I pulled out of it today. I saved one cake, so I ate it today, and Darling, it was really swell. Raught and Lingis said to thank you very much for the eats.

Well, the way things look now there's no possible chance of us getting a furlough, but I didn't expect any. I'm sure glad you came down to see me. I don't think I would have been able to go across in very good spirits if I hadn't gotten to see you.

That was a nice dream you had the other night. Let's hope it really comes true in the near future. Darling, it really will be wonderful when we're married. We won't have to use park benches then. Ha! If I get back from overseas in one piece you can bet your last dollar that we'll get married. I don't know what we'll live on, but I guess we'll get along some way.

It doesn't seem possible that we've been engaged for five months. It just doesn't seem that long. Maybe it won't be so very long before we can celebrate a wedding anniversary.

You're so sweet, Darling, and believe me when I say I love you with all my heart.

All My Love, Darling, for You,

Bob

—— —— ——·—— ——/ ——···——/·——·/·——··/··/——·/—— ——·/

June 24, 1944, 6 am

My Darling Francs,

I hope you don't have too much trouble reading this as I'm flying right now. Vital statistics--Air Speed 175 MPH, Altitude 23,000 Ft.

Radio Silence. We're on our graduation hop today. There are 100 planes in the formation, and we're headed for Tampa, Florida. Ordinarily I'd be working like hell right now, but today all ships keep radio silence except the lead ship. I figure I'm lucky to be able to fly. Flying is something that is hard to explain. Darling, it gets under your skin. I feel 100% better the minute the ship leaves the ground.

Darling, I miss you something terrible. Sometimes I think we should have gotten married. But I guess we did the right thing in waiting till I come back from combat. I do want to see our children grow up, and when we get married, I want to be with you all the time. You are the only one I've ever loved.

I want to be able to give you a big kiss in the morning when I leave, and a bigger one when I get home at night.

With All My Love and More,

Bob

---.--/ -...-/.-./.-../../-./--./

July 13, 1944

My Darling Frances,

I am now in a staging area, to be exact, Hunter Field, Savannah, Geo. We got here around 11:00 this morning. They tell us we'll be here less than a week. It's a pretty sure thing we'll get a plane here to fly over. Darling, if I go to England, I'll say in my letter that it's the place I expected to go. If it's the South Pacific, I'll say they sent us where I didn't think we'd go. If it's India, I'll say it's the place I least expected to go. If it's Italy, I'll say it's the place where they don't serve warm beer. If they send me to Alaska, I'll drop dead! Ha!

All My Love, Darling, Forever,

Bob

---·--/ -···-/·-·/·-··/··/-·/--·/

Gulfport Army Airfield was 100 percent better than the Dalhart base, according to Bob. The airplanes were relatively new and in excellent condition. At the conclusion of the crew's training in Gulfport, they were shipped to Savannah, Georgia, where they were issued a new B-17G bomber to fly overseas for combat duty. Secrecy and security became of paramount importance. Bob was limited in what information he could convey to Frances. Letters sent to the United States from military personnel in combat zones were censored. None of Bob's letters appear to have been censored, but it must have been eerie to know your letter would be read by someone else in addition to its intended recipient.

---·--/ -···-/·-·/·-··/··/-·/--·/

July 15, 1944

My Darling Frances,

Monday we'll get our airplane and take it up for a few hours to see if it flies O.K. Tuesday we leave here in our plane. Where we are going from here, I do not know, and if I did know I couldn't tell you. They gave us more equipment than I ever thought possible for one man to keep track of, including a .45 automatic. If I get to the other side without losing any of it, it will be a miracle.

Our whole crew went to town yesterday on an overnight pass. We had two large rooms at the Hotel DeSoto in Savannah. We had a good time. Most of the crew had a pretty good edge on including me and all the officers. We kinda let ourselves go because we knew that it would be the last chance we'd be able to have a party like that in a long time.

All My Love to My Darling Wife,

Bob

---·--/ -···-/·-·/·-··/··/-·/--·/

July 26, 1944

My Darling Frances,

I can't tell you where I am, but I can tell you that I'm in one of the New England states. This is the first time I've been able to write in about a week. I'm not too sure that I will get to mail this or if it will get through or not. I'm sitting in the radio room of our ship writing this and looking at your picture. It sure has been lonely not hearing from you and knowing that I won't till I reach my destination. It's my time to sleep in the ship tonight. It has to be guarded at all times, and tonight is my night to sleep in it. I usually dream when I sleep in the ship, and I'm praying tonight that I dream about you. I'm anxious to get over there and get it over with so I can get back in a hurry and change your name to mine.

All My Love, Darling, for You,

Bob

---·--/ -···-/·-·/·-··/··/-·/--·/

August 2, 1944

My Darling Frances,

I'm somewhere in Newfoundland, but, naturally, I can't tell you where. I, also, can't tell you where I'm going from here or how long I'll be here. In fact, there's not much I can tell you. When I reach my final destination, I'll write you a long letter.

All My Love, Darling, for You,

Bob

---.--/ -...-/.-./.-../../-./--./

Bob's stateside training had lasted one year, ten months, and nine days. He and the rest of the B-17 crew flew out for the European theater on July 28, 1944, arriving in Italy on August 6, 1944. They first flew to Bangor, Maine, then to Gander Bay, Newfoundland, next to the Azores, Portugal, on to Marrakesh, Morocco, and then across the Sahara Desert to Tunis, Tunisia, and finally to Foggia, Italy, to join up with the 97th Bombardment Group, 340th Bomb Squadron of the Fifteenth Army Air Force.

Venit Hora – The Hour Has Come

Motto of the 97th Bombardment Group

Chapter Nine

The Flying Fortress

The B-17 Bomber. The Queen of the Skies, The Flying Fortress

"The B-17, I think, was the best combat airplane ever built. It combined in perfect balance the right engine, the right wing, and the right control surfaces. The B-17 was a bit more rugged than the B-24. It could ditch better because of the low wing, and it could sustain more battle damage. You wouldn't believe they could stay in the air."

—Lieutenant General Ira C. Eaker,
Commander of the Eighth Air Force and
Deputy Commander of the United States Army Air Forces

"The B-17 was as tough an airplane as was ever built. It was a good honest plane to fly—a pilot's airplane. It did everything it was asked to do and did it well."

—*General Curtis E. LeMay,*
Chief of Staff of the United States Air Force

"By far the best bomber we had in the war. I'd rather have the B-17 than any other. Without the B-17 we might have lost the war."

—*General Carl A. Spaatz,*
Commander of Strategic Air Forces in Europe

The B-17 bomber became the most celebrated and widely known airplane of WWII. It dropped more bombs in WWII than any other aircraft. Of the 1.5 million tons of bombs dropped during the war, 640,000 tons were dropped by B-17s. The most famous B-17 bomber was the *Memphis Belle*. Flying in the Eighth Air Force out of England, the crew of the *Memphis Belle* completed their required 25 missions on May 17, 1943. They were one of the first bomber crews to finish the difficult task. After its 25 missions, the *Memphis Belle* toured America promoting War Bonds. The Army Air Force produced a documentary film in 1944 about the aircraft, *The Memphis Belle: A Story of a Flying Fortress.*

This publicity brought home to America what it was like to fly missions over enemy territory in a B-17. Well, at least some of the more glamorous aspects. Before December 1943, only 30 percent of bomber crews completed their 25 missions. A total of 12,731 B-17s were manufactured from 1935-45. Of these, 4,750 Flying Fortresses, or almost 40 percent, were lost on combat missions. The bomber command leaders were willing to accept this amount of loss of men and planes to destroy a major strategic target.

Unlike England, which developed a bomber defense system during the Battle of Britain, Germany considered such a defense system unnecessary. The Germans were not impressed with the Allies' air war, and they did not see the long-range bombers as a threat in the early stages of the war. It was a judgement error that cost them dearly later. Even as late as August 1943, the German Air Minister Goering refused to look at Air Ministry reports on Allied bombing statistics, calling it all enemy propaganda. Hitler was also delusional about the Allied bomber reports, calling them "planted stories" meant to confuse the German Air Ministry. The German high command was also unrealistic in believing that the Allied bombers could be stopped by their Luftwaffe forces before they entered Germany. These and other false assumptions and decisions worked in favor of the Allies slowly winning air superiority.

Even so, the Luftwaffe continued to inflict terrible losses on the American and British bombers in Western Europe. The Germans also countered with increased defensive measures, most notably, increasing the number of flak guns, particularly around the key German military targets. As Allied bombers approached their targets, flak shells exploded around the planes. The bombers had no defense against flak. It was simply a matter of luck whether you survived or not, even in a Flying Fortress.

A Mass-Production Marvel

In the Boeing Building at The National WWII Museum in New Orleans, Louisiana, a B-17 bomber hangs suspended from the ceiling. When a visitor walks in the door and looks up, the B-17 bomber, named *My Gal Sal*, has its 103-foot, 8.9-inch wingspan stretching all the way across the top of the structure. Spanning the building from front to back is the plane's body, 73 feet, 8.9 inches long. The B-17 is an impressive sight from any angle. It was designed to be a long-range bomber that could carry a heavy bomb load and bomb from high altitudes with precision. One of the keys to the B-17's success was that it could be mass produced. Its parts were interchangeable, making the bomber easier to service and repair. Thousands of modifications were made to the B-17 from the A model to the G model, but the basic design did not change.

The ability of the U.S. industry to reach production levels that no other country could match gave a decisive advantage to the Allies in the closing years of the war. While Germany's aircraft industry was dealing with relentless attacks from Allied bombing, the United States aircraft industry reached maximum production of 130 B-17Gs a week, or twice the weekly loss rate. Each B-17 cost $270,000 to produce.

As Jay Stout wrote in *The Men Who Killed the Luftwaffe*, "By January 1944, American industry was just hitting its stride; factories in the United States were producing quantities of aircraft that greatly exceeded what Germany or any other nation manufactured."

An American Workhorse and A Team of Men

The B-17 was the workhorse of the WWII American bombing effort. It was easy to fly, stable, and quick to respond. Possibly its best quality was its ability to absorb punishment and survive attacks. Many B-17s endured seemingly hopeless structural damage to bring their airmen home. Tales abounded of miraculous landings with only one engine working, plane noses shot off, or belly landings. No wonder their crews held the B-17 in reverence. Even so, flying in a B-17 was no luxury trip.

Flying missions at altitudes of 20,000 to 30,000 feet meant that the temperatures could be -20 to -40 degrees Fahrenheit in the B-17. Frostbite was a constant danger, especially if an airman was wounded. To fight this cold, crews were issued electrically heated suits and a second heavy flight suit. The breech locks on the machine guns had electric heaters to prevent the mechanisms from freezing.

Fortunately for Bob, he was in the radio room, the relatively warmest area in the aircraft. He never wore an electrically heated suit. The gunners in the rear of the craft—the coldest area—always wore them. One problem with a heated suit was there were hot spots and areas that did not work due to faulty wiring. Bob protected himself from the cold temperatures with three layers of clothing, including a wool coat worn over his flight suit. Oxygen masks had to be worn at altitudes over 10,000 feet in a B-17. An airman could die from lack of oxygen. The oxygen system could fail or be damaged in combat. Oxygen masks could freeze up. In the frenzy of battle, a crewman might not notice that his oxygen mask was not working. The B-17, despite its large size, is a cramped aircraft on the inside. It was tight and awkward to move around in the small spaces, and maneuverability was further hampered by the heavy clothing worn by the crews to keep them warm. It was an uncomfortable, cold, dangerous, and long ride.

As Bob recalled, "When we approached altitudes of 10,000 feet and above, we had to wear oxygen masks. It would get uncomfortable because we'd have to wear them for four or five hours at a time. Then you had the cold temperatures. We didn't have pressurized and insulated cabins like they have now. Sometimes your mask would ice up and you'd have to take it off and beat it against something to get the ice out of it and put it back on."

Also important to remember, is that all the systems in a B-17 were mechanical. There were no electronic calculators or electronic systems. From the telegraph key, invented in 1844, that the radio operator used to tap out Morse code, to the arming of the bombs carried in the B-17 belly, all systems were mechanical. Hydraulics, the mechanical function that operates through the force of liquid pressure, powered the landing gear, wing flaps, fuel, and other systems. It is hard to imagine in a world of computerized precision and speed that a complicated airplane worked entirely by mechanical systems dependent on the skills and knowledge of its crew, who were not professional airmen.

"The miracle was that the Air Force had taken thousands of civilians and transformed them into pilots, one of the most exacting occupations known to man. Men who had never flown before were somehow taught to be fliers who were given the most advanced aircraft up to that time and then took them out to take part in extremely complex operations. This in itself was no simple job. The Army Air Force, particularly, pioneered new teaching methods which resulted in remarkably capable airmen. This applied also to the ground crews, also mainly ex-civilians who were given the job of keeping the most complicated machines in existence in combat condition."

"These civilians, part-time warriors, led by the professionals without whom they would have been lost, went about their daily work as if hazard and heroics were common commodities. They had never flown before and, after the war ended, many never flew again. But while they were airborne, they performed epical deeds."

The B-17 was manned by a crew of ten well-trained men. The crew became more than a working team. They became a family. The perils and fears of flying missions bound them together. The average age of a B-17 crew member was 22 and over half were teenagers. The highest possible physical standards were required of the crew.

Bob's Crew. Bob pictured front row, 3rd from the left.

All ten crewmen in a B-17 were placed into situations they had never been in or dreamed of being in before. Whatever their position in the plane, each man was trained to do a specific job with additional side responsibilities. For example, the bombardier, the navigator, the engineer, and the radio operators were also gunners. In times of crisis during a mission, crewmen helped out wherever they were needed.

No B-17 could fly without its ground crew. Whatever it took, however long it took, the ground crews kept the B-17s flying. The crew of eight to ten mechanics per plane worked outdoors or in makeshift shelters in good and bad weather, night and day, to keep the planes flying. The plane belonged to the chief of the ground crew, not to the pilot or the air crew. It was the chief who took care of the plane. He and his crew patched the holes, did the maintenance, and kept the plane in the best flying condition possible.

Along with mechanical crews, staggering numbers of people and equipment kept the bombers flying. Only fifteen percent of the United States Army Air Force were pilots and crews. Added to this difficult logistics puzzle, every piece of military equipment and personnel had to be shipped across the Atlantic Ocean or the Pacific Ocean to Army Air Force bases.

"To put 500 bombers in the air demanded a backup of 75,000 officers and men, 300 tons of operational equipment, plus fuel and bombs, and a standing reserve of 85,000 tons of spare parts."

Bob and his crew were assigned a new B-17G model in July 1944. It was the last model of the B-17 bomber that was manufactured.

Details of the positions of Bob's B-17 air crew, from the front to the back of the airplane:

The Bombardier
2nd Lt. Eugene Anderson, from Wisconsin

The nose of a B-17 is a very modern looking, clear plexiglass bubble. The bombardier was stationed here. What a view he had! Starting in some of the B-17F models, a chin turret armed with two .50-caliber machine guns was added under the plexiglass nose. One of the B-17's defensively weak spots was the front nose area. The German fighter pilots quickly figured this out, and they attacked the B-17s from the front, head on. This required a great deal of skill from the German attacker coming straight on at 400 miles per hour. Done to precision, it was lethal to the B-17 bomber. To counter this vulnerable point, the chin turret was added. All the G models were equipped with this new gun turret that the bombardier fired when not executing his job as the bombardier.

The bombardier operated the "top secret" precision Norden bombsight. Bombardiers took an oath to destroy the Norden bombsight rather than have it end up in German hands. The Norden bombsight was created by a Dutch engineer, Carl Lucas Norden. It was the most sophisticated non-electronic aiming device ever created. It could direct bombs to hit within a 50-foot radius from an altitude of more than 20,000 feet. "This precision compensated for the plane's forward motion, drift, movement of the target; it computed automatically what would have taken a man many minutes."

The Norden bombsight was accurate under ideal conditions, but ideal conditions were not often obtainable in the skies over enemy territory. The bombardier was operating a very sophisticated piece of machinery that required precise data to be fed into the mechanism. Under battle fire from flak and enemy fighters, plus variable weather conditions, precise data was not possible. The Norden bombsight was the best one available, but its precision was compromised in actual battle.

When the B-17 made its final approach over the target, the plane was put on autopilot until the bombs were released, with the bombardier in control of the airplane during the actual bomb run. He was flying the airplane through the connections between his Norden bombsight and the autopilot system. This made the B-17s sitting ducks for the flak gunners below because the planes could not deviate from their flight path until the bombs were dropped. As soon as "bombs away" was uttered, the plane came off autopilot and evasive flying was returned to the pilot and co-pilot to get out of the plane's dangerous position.

Bombardier's Oath

> *"Mindful of the secret trust about to be placed in me by my Commander in Chief, the President of The United States, by whose direction I have been chosen for bombardier training, and mindful of the fact that I am to become guardian of one of my country's most priceless military assets, the American bombsight, I do here, in the presence of Almighty God, swear by the Bombardier's Code of Honor to keep inviolate the secrecy of any and all confidential information revealed to me, and further to uphold the honor and integrity of the Army Air Forces, if need be, with my life itself."*

The Navigator

1st Lt. Gus Iverson, from New Jersey

The navigator's station was behind the bombardier in the nose of the plane. He operated from a small desk that was located on the left side of the nose area. The navigator's job was to plot the routes the plane would take to and from the target. Sounds easy enough until you run into enemy fighter planes, bad weather, flak, or you fall out of formation. Then it got dicey.

After attending target briefings for the day, "Navigators would pick up their charts and logs, plot the route to and from the target and alternative target, the estimated time of arrival at assembly points, turning points, initial points, targets, the predicted winds, and weather along the way. All done, they packed up and double-checked that they had everything in their briefcases, charts and flight plan, EGB computer (manually operated and nothing like modern electronics), protractor and dividers, weather card, code data sheets, and several sharpened pencils."

The navigator calculated everything the old-fashioned way, with paper and pencil, and without the aid of calculators or computers. Written in The Pilot Training Manual for the B-17, the four methods the navigator could use to determine the position of the airplane in regard to the earth were listed as dead reckoning; radio, working closely with the radio operator; celestial navigation using stars and planets; or pilotage, the method of determining the airplane's position by visual reference to the ground. In the final analysis, it was the navigator's best educated guess to determine the route the plane should take. When B-17s were flying in formation, the navigator could rely on the lead navigator in the lead airplane to calculate the way for the whole formation.

After bombs were dropped, formations often fell apart. Then it was up to the navigator to give his pilots the information needed to get the plane on the quickest course home, all while being attacked by flak guns and enemy fighter planes. If the plane had received damage on the bombing run, the job was even more difficult.

The navigator was also a gunner. He fired a .50-caliber machine gun that was mounted to the right side of the plane behind the plexiglass nose tip.

The Pilot and Copilot

1st Lt. Josie Folz, pilot, from Virginia
2nd Lt. Dennis Birke, co-pilot, from Texas

Behind the nose of the B-17 and sitting higher up in the cockpit were the pilot and copilot. They could see above, forward, and to the sides, but they could not see the earth beneath them or the plane and sky behind them. Over 150 instruments were arranged around the cockpit. The B-17 was the most complicated airplane of its day, and the pilots had to know it thoroughly.

Someone had to be in charge, and that was the pilot. He was the commander of the ship. He made the decisions that determined the fate of the plane and the nine other crewmen, based on the information he received from the rest of the crew, plus his own perspective on the airplane's ability to fly. He often had to make split-second decisions. The job of the pilot and copilot was to fly the ship, and it was a joint effort. Some missions involved ten hours of flying time, so the pilot and copilot shared the flying responsibilities. In some situations, it took the strength of both men to fly the plane. For instance, it took two men to pull a B-17 out of a dive and, often, two men to pilot a wounded plane home.

Their responsibilities weighed heavily on bomber pilots. An Army Air Force profile of the ideal bomber pilot concluded, "Bomber pilots suffered much higher casualties than fighter pilots, and with greater responsibilities as crew commander, they were more susceptible to mental breakdowns or combat fatigue."

The best way to knock out a B-17 was to kill the pilots. Therefore, it was important to stay in formation, which required the pilots to always be attentive to their position in the formation. This was exhausting, but there was safety in numbers. A plane listing out of its position could cause a mid-air collision, and a plane that fell out of formation was an easy target for enemy fighters. Amazingly, often without any prior flying experience before the war, these pilots successfully flew the big B-17s on their missions. Yes, there were heavy losses, especially early in the strategic bombing campaign, but most planes were successfully piloted home.

Engineer

T/Sgt. Dalton Cormier, from Louisiana

The engineer was in charge of maintaining every system in the plane. The systems included electrical, hydraulic, heating, flight controls, oxygen, fuel, engines, bombs, and guns. He was the maintenance crewman in the sky, and he had to have an extensive knowledge of the workings of the plane. When there was damage, the engineer was charged with making repairs. If the ball turret stuck, it was the engineer who fixed it. If the landing gear malfunctioned, it was the engineer who repaired it. In short, he was the handyman for everything on the plane. During flight, the engineer stood between the pilots or sat in the jump seat behind the pilots. He assisted the pilots with monitoring the mechanical workings of the plane. On take-offs and landings, the engineer called out the air speed.

In addition to these overwhelming responsibilities, the engineer manned the top turret guns. The top turret was a critical gun position. The engineer stood in the turret with his head and shoulders in a plexiglass bubble above the plane with two .50-caliber machine guns. He had a spectacular view of the top of the plane and of the horizon for a full 360 degrees. The engineer had the best opportunity to knock out enemy fighters who were flying head-on to destroy the B-17. From his view above the plane, the engineer could visually check out any damage to the wings, engines, and the outside top of the airplane. He also had a great view of all that was occurring in the skies above the plane.

Bomb-bay Area

Behind the engineer was the bomb-bay area, where the bombs were loaded and released over the target. "Bomb-bay racks were fitted to carry a wide variety of bombs, ranging from 100-pound to 2,000-pound bombs. External bomb racks were installed under the wings but were not used with any frequency. Maximum bomb load restricted the B-17's range, so a careful balance was always struck between bomb load and fuel supply."

Radio Operator
T/Sgt. Robert Oakes, from Indiana

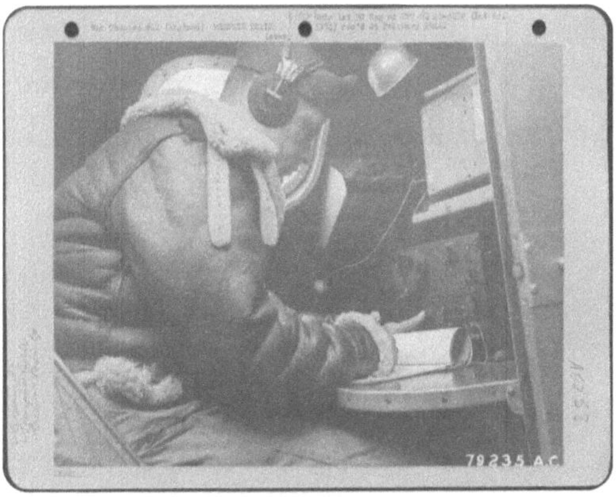

Radio Operator at his station in B17 during World War II.

Behind the bomb-bay was the radio room. As the only area in the plane that had a door at the front and a door at the back of the space, it was really a room inside the plane, located where the wings and fuselage connected. It was structurally one of the strongest parts of the airplane. The B-17 was a noisy plane, so the enclosed radio room gave the radio operator a quieter space to hear incoming messages and Morse code.

The radio room was the communications hub of the airplane. It was equipped with a surprisingly advanced system of communication, with the capability of using both Morse code and voice. The long-distance communications system, the Liaison Radio, provided for long-range communication between the aircraft and ground stations. Distress calls and long-range mission progress signals were sent through this channel. Escort fighter planes and bomber planes communicated with each other using VHF Command Radio with a range of about 150 miles. The Command Radio provided short-range voice communication with other aircraft or the ground within 30 miles.

Along with these two systems, there was a communication system for the crew to speak to each other. The radio operator often worked closely with the navigator to calculate the plane's route, especially by obtaining directional coordinates to reach home base. Radio signals sent from Allied radio beacons could give the navigator the plane's position. The radio operator had to know the electronic workings of his receivers, transmitters, and equipment. In addition, he had to know how to repair them. The radio operator's duties also included sending in a strike report containing the time the bombs were released and an explanation of the visual results of the attack, all in Morse code. He was also the main first-aid man and operated a .50-caliber machine gun, which was located above the radio room.

Ball Turret Gunner
S/Sgt. John Lawson, from Wyoming

Perhaps the most unusual position in a B-17 was the ball turret. It was located behind the radio room in the floor of the fuselage. The ball turret was a 43-inch diameter steel sphere that electrically operated and could be moved in many directions. "The ball turret could be moved very quickly, and proved to be an operational success, exacting a heavy toll on the enemy."

The entry hatch into the ball turret was behind the gunner's back. This required another crew member to get him into and out of the round turret when the plane was in flight. With the turret guns pointing straight down, the hatch could be opened, and the ball turret gunner could slip into the restricted space. Then the hatch above him was locked tight. If the pilot ordered the crew to bail, the ball turret gunner had to hope someone would help him get out.

The tiny, cramped space required a man of small stature to fit in it. There wasn't even room for the ball turret gunner's parachute to fit in the tight space. He had to keep his parachute outside of the ball turret in the fuselage of the plane. The ball turret gunner was also exposed to extreme cold. Just as the top turret gunner had a great view of the sky and the top of the plane, the ball turret gunner had a great view of the underside of the plane and all that was below.

In the ball turret, the gunner could move in many directions, offering a panoramic view. He had two .50-caliber machine guns to operate with gun sights between his feet. The ball turret gunner operated the turret and his two guns using both feet and both hands. Imagine flying in this extremely cold, cramped, claustrophobic space for sometimes up to 10 hours!

Waist Gunners

S/Sgt. Charles Gleason, from New York
S/Sgt. Clifton Huffman, from West Virginia

The belly of the B-17 housed two waist gunners, one on each side of the plane. Each had a great view of the action on their side of the plane. When the gunners stood and fired their guns, their backs nearly touched.

Each waist gunner fired a .50-caliber machine gun. The guns were equipped with their own heating system to keep them warm enough to fire. That's how cold it was in the open-air space with wind whipping in the windows. Keeping his gun operational was a critical job for a gunner, both during a mission and on the ground. The guns had to be cleaned and thoroughly inspected for damage and wear after each mission. The survival of the crew often depended on the gunners' ability to shoot down enemy fighters.

"But regardless of the fact that it is impossible to precisely measure the number of German aircraft shot down by the gunners aboard the heavy bombers, there is no debating the fact that they were effective to a very great extent. Although the gunners put in claims for more aircraft than they actually destroyed, they did shoot down significant numbers of German fighters."

Scanning the skies to spot enemy fighters attacking the bomber was another job for the gunners. They had to be constantly vigilant. The waist gunners worked in a cramped and very cold space. Their bulky suits and multiple layers of gloves made the manipulation of their weapons even more difficult.

The Tail Gunner
S/Sgt. Richard Leonard, from Ohio

The first B-17 models were not equipped with a tail gunner position, but this was quickly modified. The tail of the plane was a very vulnerable spot for enemy attacks, making the tail gunner position one of the most dangerous places in the plane. The tail gunner protected the plane from rear attacks. He kept the pilot informed of what he could see of the formation behind. He operated two .50-caliber machine guns. The tail gunner worked in a very cold, very cramped space, sitting on a seat that was shaped like a bicycle seat.

His position was tenuous as "the tail gunner hunched, facing backwards in his tortuously cramped compartment underneath the plane's soaring tail section. His windowed space was so tight that his twin guns had to be fed by an ammunition track that led to storage magazines in the middle of the ship."

To get to his battle station, the tail gunner had to crawl through the back of the tight, claustrophobic fuselage. Of all the positions, the tail gunner was the most likely to die of anoxia, or lack of oxygen, due to his solitary position in the plane's tail. Isolated from the rest of the crew, and more vulnerable to attack, the tail gunner carried out his job to protect the rear of the plane.

Ten men comprised the B-17 Flying Fortress crew with whom Bob was assigned. Their shared experiences in combat and in down times forged them together. They became a closely bonded fighting unit.

"The equipment of survival both tightened and symbolized this bond. Ten men were linked to the ship and to one another by hose lines and wires, hoses to keep them breathing, wires to keep them in touch with one another."

Chapter Ten

Scared All the Time

By 1943, the Army Air Force had flying divisions stationed all over the world. In June 1944, Bob and his crew were assigned to the Fifteenth Army Air Force, 97th Bombardment Group, 340th Bomb Squadron. The Fifteenth Army Air Force Division was stationed in southern Italy, where the Allies had defeated the Nazi forces. The Germans had retreated up the Italian peninsula into the northern part of Italy, where ground fighting continued. Heavy bombers and fighter planes were needed to fly missions out of Italy, due to its proximity to enemy territory.

The Fifteenth Army Air Force soon became an effective weapon against the enemy's oil refineries, factories, and transportation hubs. The heavy bombers and fighter planes were also used to support the Allied troops fighting on the ground. Bob was suddenly in one of the most dangerous places in WWII, dropping bombs over enemy land.

Being assigned to the newly constructed airfield in Foggia, Italy, was another important factor for Bob's survival. The field, rough as it was, made bombing deep in enemy territory a much shorter trip than from England or North Africa. The difficulty in flying north out of Italy was that the Alps Mountain Range had to be crossed coming and going. The B-17 could easily clear the Alps, but for an injured B-17 or one low on fuel coming home from a bombing run, the Alps could be problematic.

Bob arrived at the air base near Foggia on August 6, 1944, and immediately began flying missions to Germany and German-occupied territories in southeastern Europe.

Bob was 22, and Frances was 19.

–––·––/ –···–/·–·/·–··/··/–·/––·/

August 8, 1944

My Darling Frances,

I haven't been able to get my mail as yet, but we're supposed to in the next couple of days. I don't mind telling you I could use a letter from you pretty bad. I'm somewhere in Italy. I can't tell you where. I feel fine except that I'm pretty dirty, but I think I'll get to take a good bath today. It's a little rough right now, but it's a lot better than being stuck back at Gulfport.

When I talk to an Italian, I have to do it all with my hands. When I get back and start to talking with my arms and hands don't think I'm going crazy.

Darling, I don't have to tell you how much I miss you because you know. I won't have to tell you how much I love you because you know that too. As soon as I get back, we're going to get married.

All My Love, Darling, for You,

Bob

–––·––/ –···–/·–·/·–··/··/–·/––·/

August 9, 1944

My Darling Frances,

I'm still in Italy. I'm living in a tent, but it's fixed up pretty nice and not a bit bad. I don't know how long it will be before I'll get any mail, but it can't be too soon to suit me. I sure need a letter from you bad, but I guess I'll have to wait. I don't think it will take long to get my missions in, and then I'll be back and you know what will happen then.

I think I'll have time to write pretty regularly if I can find enough material to write with. It's just about time for chow, so I guess I better get on it. I'm the type that doesn't miss that.

Darling, I love you with all my heart. Just wait awhile, and I'll be back.

All My Love, Darling,

Bob

−−−·−−/ −···−/·−·/·−··/··/−·/−−·/

August 11, 1944

My Darling Frances,

Another day and it brings me a day closer to you, which doesn't make me unhappy. I don't know how long it will be before I get back to you, but I'll be counting the days, no matter how many it is.

Have everything ready, Darling, so we can get married as soon as I come home. Just think, I'll get 30 whole days at home. Won't that be wonderful? I guess I'm just a little ahead of myself, but I don't think it will do any harm to look into the future.

I hope the censor doesn't chop anything out of this letter, because I'm writing on both sides of the paper, but I don't think he'll cut anything out.

I finally made another stripe, and now I am a sergeant. it means one thing to me, more money. Tell your mother I said hello, and I'd sure like to have some of HER gravy. I love you with all my heart, and I'm sweating this war out, but I think I'll make it OK.

All My Love, Darling, for You,

Bob

---·--/ -···-/·-·/·-··/··/-·/--·/

August 18, 1944

My Darling Frances,

I thought they kept me pretty busy in the states, but they were playing compared to over here. I got down from flying the other day and had several letters waiting for me. They were the first I had gotten since I've been overseas. I don't have to tell you how much that helped my morale. I thought I'd have tomorrow off and would have plenty of time to write letters. But I don't, so I'm forced to write this by candlelight. Darling, your letters mean everything to me. When you tell me how much you love me, I go sky high with happiness, and my heart is filled with pride because I know you're mine. You just wait awhile, Darling, and I'll be back before so very long.

Well, Darling, the candle is getting very low, and I'm getting very sleepy. I have lots to talk about, but I'd rather wait till I get home. Darling, remember I love you with all my heart.

All My Love, Darling, for You,

Bob

---·--/ -···-/·-·/·-··/··/-·/--·/

"When we first got over there the crews would be split up," Bob remembered. "They did that so we would all get experience. They'd put a pilot in a different plane for instance. My crew's copilot and waist gunner were shot down over Yugoslavia pretty early on. They were lucky, because they ended up around locals who helped them, and they made it back to the base in Italy."

---·--/ -···-/·-·/·-··/··/-·/--·/

August 22, 1944

My Darling Frances,

I saw an Italian town for the first time today, and it turned out to be quite an adventure. I really enjoyed the last letter I received from you, the one in which you reminisced a couple of instances we had some time ago. All I did the night I received your letter was think about some of the things we did and all the wonderful times we had together.

As usual I feel fine, a little tired, but outside of that I'm in top shape. I hope they're not working you too hard at the Army Depot. I suppose as long as you and Bax are together they won't work you too hard.

The longer I stay away from you, Darling, the more I love you, if that's possible. I'm living on all the memories of us together, and a person couldn't live better. I know that after this war I'm going to be very happy, and it will be all your fault. Now aren't you ashamed of yourself? I'll try very hard to write to you tomorrow if I can possibly find the time at all.

All My Love to You, Sweet,

Bob

---·--/ -···-/·-·/·-··/··/-·/--·/

Frances quit college and, like many women during that time, worked for the war effort. She had taken a job in the nearby town of Jeffersonville, Indiana, at the Jeffersonville Quartermaster Depot. The Depot served as a shipping station for military supplies that were sent to military stations and combat zones. Frances was assigned to the Depot office to schedule and manage shipments. She had given up her dreams of college and a career, but with Bob in combat, she knew that she had to help the war effort. To her and many Americans, this was an easy choice. With men enlisting to fight, many jobs were filled for the first time with women, who more than proved their worth.

---·--/ -···-/·-·/·-··/··/-·/--·/

August 26, 1944

My Darling Frances,

I received a letter from you today addressed to my new A.P.O. It took 9 days for it to get here, which isn't too bad. I got five others from you that were mailed to the old A.P.O.#, which made me get lots of mail today, and that always makes me happy.

Tell the girls at the Depot that I really enjoyed their letters. The only regret I have is that I'm not there to collect all of their kisses.

I'm very sorry to hear your Grandpa died, but I suppose it was for the better. I imagine it rather upset things.

I took time out for supper. I hope you didn't mind. I'm now officially a sergeant. They told me I was one about a week ago, but there was a mix up, and actually I wasn't. Everything is straightened out now, and I'm officially a sergeant.

I got a crew cut haircut the other day, and do I look rough, like hell. I don't have to comb it anymore, which means a lot. It'll be all grown out by the time I get home, I hope.

It hasn't been long since I last saw you, but it seems like it has been years. The war can't last forever. When it's over I'll make up for lost time. Take care of yourself, Darling, and I'll try very hard to write tomorrow.

I Send All My Love to You Alone,

Bob

P.S. I'd sure like to be with you tonight.

---·--/ -···-/·-·/·-··/··/-·/--·/

The raids on the Ploiesti, Romania, oil refineries proved especially devasting to the German military. "The Eighth and the Fifteenth joined on August 24, 1944, for combined raids on the oil plants. All oil production ceased, and the plant was occupied by the Soviets a few days later." This was a loss of 40 percent of all the oil Germany needed to wage war. In these raids, the British bombers and United States Fifteenth Army Air Force, including Bob's bomber group, suffered a far higher loss rate than the Eighth Army Air Force had throughout the summer of 1944. Bob flew two missions over Ploiesti, which was one of the most dangerous destinations to bomb. The fuel produced at Ploiesti was critical to the German war machine, so the oil plant was fortified and protected with an extra number of flak guns and German fighter planes.

---·--/ -···-/·-·/·-··/··/-·/--·/

August 31, 1944

My Darling Frances,

Excuses are in order for my lacking in writing for the last 2 or 3 days, but I'm going to fool you and not make any excuses.

Whenever you send any packages to me see if you can find a good book and send it. I think in the future I'll have plenty of time to read.

Today is payday, but that doesn't mean anything as there is no place to spend it. I guess that's pretty good, because we'll need all the money that I can get my hands on, and probably a little more. Darling, I can hardly wait till I get back to the states, because from then on, I'm going to be the happiest man in the world. Sometimes I don't see how I live without you. At times I don't see how the boys in the tent live with me, because I get awful hard to live with. I know it's all going to turn out OK in the end.

All My Love, Darling, for You,

Bob

---·--/ -···-/·-·/·-··/··/-·/--·/

September 4, 1944

My Darling Frances,

I've been receiving mail every other day pretty regular, but it's always screwed up. I'll get two letters and one will have been mailed 5 days earlier, and that's the way it always comes.

I've won an air medal, but I haven't been officially notified about it as yet. But there is no way they can possibly screw me out of it.

Darling, I don't care how many baby pictures of me you look at. If I remember correctly, they are a lot better than the grown-up ones. I hope our children take after their mother instead of their father. I know one thing for sure. Our children will have the best mother in the world.

She's the most understanding, the sweetest, and most lovable Mother a person could find in the whole wide world. If our children take after their mother, they will be tops. They'll be wonderful. I know that they can't be anything else with a mother like you.

Darling, I'm sure glad you mentioned the September 2 date. I had forgotten all about it, and when you mentioned it, it started me to thinking. It seems like September 2, 1940 was twenty years ago instead of four. I sure didn't dream that I would be in Italy now. Those four years, Darling, have been the happiest four years of my life. I wasn't sure you were mine those four years, but being near you was enough consolation. I live for the day I can once again take you in my arms and kiss you like the last time we were together.

The Whole Sky Full of My Love,

Bob

---.--/ -...-/.-./.-../../-./--./

This is what Frances wrote in her diary on September 2, 1940:

Dear Diary,

Today I slept pretty late to this afternoon. Daddy took Marilyn, Betty, and I riding. Mother went later with us. We went to the Colonial Club and then to the Country Club and saw the boys and they suggested a party so they met here and we ended up at Shine's.

There were Bob S. and Betty and Gene and Peggy, George and Betty F. and Bob and I. No one had a car so we all walked. We had lots of fun.

That's All, Frances

Not exactly revealing. Perhaps it was their first kiss or a declaration of love. Whatever happened, it was a turning point in their relationship, a day they both remembered as a special moment in their lives, with a love that lasted a lifetime, through the war, through bad times, and through good times.

---·--/ -···-/·-·/·-··/··/-·/--·/

September 6, 1944

My Darling Frances,

I couldn't find time to write to you yesterday, but I have lots of time today. I'll try to make up for missing yesterday.

My whole crew has been playing poker ever since payday including me. I finally got tired of playing and sent my money home, or should I say bought a money order. My luck wasn't too good. I broke just about even after all the smoke had cleared. I saved $70.00 dollars out of this month's pay.

I imagine that the war with Germany will be over before I finish my missions, but I'm about positive they'll send us to another theater, but of course you can never tell about this army. Anything can happen and usually does. Our group is receiving a presidential citation today and we have to put on a big review this afternoon much against my will and pleasure.

I can remember more incidents about us since I came overseas. Remember the time you went to a dance, but not with me, and Bax didn't go with Peaches. She went with someone else. Peaches and

I stagged it. We wouldn't dance with you and Bax for a long time. Finally, I couldn't stand it any longer and cut in. I tell you right now, I was a pretty happy guy when I got you in my arms and finished that dance. Gosh, but we used to do some silly things. I wouldn't trade them for anything in the world.

Jeanne says she can't get Chet to dry or wash dishes. I don't blame him one bit, but personally, right now, I'd like to be able to wash and dry dishes. In fact, I'd just like to see some dishes and be able to eat out of them once again.

We may be miles apart, but actually, you're right beside me and have a part in everything I do.

All My Love, Darling, Always,

Bob

---·--/ -···-/·-·/·-··/··/-·/--·/

September 8, 1944

My Darling Frances,

I got your picture today, and it wasn't damaged in any way whatsoever. I got the letter about 5 hours ago, and I've been staring at your picture 4 out of the 5 hours. I'm so proud of it. I showed it to all the boys in the tent, and they think it's wonderful. Cormier, my engineer, says you must be crazy to have anything to do with me. He seems to think I don't deserve you. I agreed with him and told him that. I consider myself the luckiest guy in the world.

That sure is a wonderful picture, Darling. It looks exactly like you, and that look you have. That's that look that use to send cold chills up and down my spine. Your hair is the way I like it best. It's really beautiful when you let it grow long.

I sure was sorry to hear about Melvin. He was a swell guy. Jackie is tops, and I sure feel sorry for her. [Melvin Brewer and his wife Jackie were friends of Bob and Frances. Melvin was deployed and killed in combat in France.] That incident, Darling, proves that our decision was the right one. A person never intends for it to happen, but in spite of all, it sometimes does.

I was glad to hear Chet got home. He sure has been lucky about getting home. I only hope the war is over before he gets into action, but I don't suppose you could tell him that. [Frances' brother, Chet, was trained as a Navy pilot in an Avenger torpedo plane, which was slow and, therefore, vulnerable to being shot down when dropping its torpedo.]

Goodnight, Darling. All My Love for You always,

Bob

---·--/ -···-/·-·/·-··/··/-·/--·/

September 11, 1944

My Darling Frances,

I've been flying combat missions ever since I've been over here. I thought I told you that, but I guess not. I have over 15 missions right now, so it won't take me too long to finish up.

Darling, I sure would love to get you a ring over here, but this country is pretty well on the rocks now, and they don't have a damn thing. You asked me what I want for Christmas, and I can't think of anything I need. I don't know what you want for Christmas, but whatever it is, I couldn't get it over here.

Darling, I dream every night about the day I can come home and we can get married. Just think 30 whole days at home together. It sure will be wonderful. I'll say one thing, we'll sure be deserving of those 30 days. Goodnight, "Sweet."

All My Love for You,

Bob

---·--/ -···-/·-·/·-··/··/-·/--·/

September 16, 1944

My Darling Frances,

Darling, I now have 17 missions with 33 to go. I don't know if you have read it in the papers, but here are a few of the targets we've hit: Ploesti, Romania; Munich, Germany; Oswichem, Poland; Vienna, Austria; Pardubice, Czechoslovakia; Lechfield, Germany; Athens, Greece.

I can't understand why you haven't received any mail from me for a week, because I write to you regularly. I guess you'll get a bunch of mail all at once.

I haven't as yet figured out how I'm going to keep warm when cold weather comes. This tent doesn't look too winterproof.

Darling, when you were a freshman in high school, you know when I had study hall in the auditorium, I wanted a date with you, but I didn't have the nerve to ask you. My but how things have changed. Ha! Goodnight my Sweet.

All My Love for You Darling,

Bob

---.--/ -...-/.-./.-../../-./--./

September 22, 1944

My Darling Frances,

Don't scold. I know that I haven't been writing regularly for the past week, but as usual, I have good excuses which I won't go in to. Ha!

I'll bet you could never guess who I got a letter from today. I didn't think you could. It was from George S. You remember him, don't you? He's somewhere in France with the ground forces with the Air Force. He started out the letter by saying that he thought he owed me a letter for a few years. He's a 1st Lt. too. It looks like everybody has gotten a commission but me. He said he was married. He married a hometown girl, one that he used to talk to me about all the time. Oh yes, he asked me if you and I were married. I'll have to answer his letter.

I got a promotion the 16th of this month. I am now a staff sergeant. Believe it or not, I think I'll make Tech Sgt. around the middle of next month. I'll keep plugging over here and one of these days I'll be back home again.

I'll bet you can't guess who I'm looking at right now. I'll tell you. It's a very, very sweet girl by the name of Frances Brown. They tell me she's going to marry some dope by the name of Bob Oakes. Confidentially, it wouldn't make me a bit mad. In fact, it would make me very, very happy.

I think they'll probably send me to rest camp in the middle of next month. They send us to the Isle of Capri. I've been told it's really nice. Maybe I'll find out before too long.

All My Love, Darling, Forever,

Bob

---·--/ -···-/·-·/·-··/··/-·/--·/

American Air Force doctors, who helped battle-fatigued bomber crews, realized that people in constant combat do not adapt or become used to life-threatening situations. Chronic anxiety and emotional disintegration increased with constant bombing missions. This same exposure and fear of the deadly direct hit affected both the bomber crews and the people being bombed. To lessen the effects of battle fatigue, bomber crews in Italy were sometimes sent to the Isle of Capri for a respite from flying missions. In Bob's case, he finally made it to the Isle of Capri 60 years later, on a trip to Italy with some members of his bomber group.

---·--/ -···-/·-·/·-··/··/-·/--·/

September 25, 1944

My Darling Frances,

I had a day off today, and it didn't make me a bit mad. We went to the show this afternoon and saw "Marriage is a Private Affair" with Lana Turner. It was pretty good, but I don't think it could ever happen to us. We had our pictures taken "Joe Air Corp" style with helmet etc. I can just see what it will look like. It wasn't my idea. The rest of the guys in the tent more or less talked me into it. Don't faint when I send you one. That is if I ever let it pass my censorship.

My pilot was promoted to 1st Lt. the other day, and he sure deserved it. He just got back from rest camp today. I don't know when they'll send me. Not for some time, I guess.

Darling, I can't wait to get back to the states, mainly to be with you again. I'm really sweating the missions, and it seems like a long old drag. Everything will be perfect when I get back. We can get married and spend 30 days together without any interruptions whatsoever. Won't it be marvelous, Darling? Just think all these years I've waited for that, and at last it's going to happen. It seems too good to be true.

How are your mother and dad? Tell them I said hello, and that I'm afraid before too many months pass by, they'll have to put up with me again.

I got a letter from Marvin today, and he said he had been home for a few days, and he talked with you. I suppose I'll write him a letter tonight.

Darling, I do miss you so very, very much. If I could just hold you in my arms for 5 minutes tonight, I'd be like a new man. Just to touch your hair and have your lips pressed to mine would be heaven for me tonight. Woman, what you don't do to me isn't worth mentioning. I can just take one glance at your picture and I start pulling my hair, because I'm not with you at this very moment.

All My Love, Sweet,

Bob

---·--/ -···-/·-·/·-··/··/-·/--·/

On days without a mission, down time included playing cards, writing letters, watching movies, and going into Foggia, where the Red Cross served coffee, donuts, and other items. On one occasion, an Italian shot an American soldier in Foggia, which led to orders for service men to only go into Foggia in pairs or groups, as well as to always carry one's .45 pistol.

---·--/ -···-/·-·/·-··/··/-·/--·/

September 27, 1944

My Darling Frances,

I received your letter of the 11th and was overjoyed, because it was the first letter I had received from you in a week or more. But the contents of the letter were the main cause of my happiness in receiving it. In case you are not certain about the letter I'm talking about, it's the one in which you were thinking about that night. Darling, I do agree with you and often. I have hoped and prayed that those were your thoughts. Our love is beautiful, and I knew that from the very start, and I have always striven to keep it that way. I knew that I'd never regret it.

Darling, as long as we've been going together, we've gotten along wonderfully. We've had a few disagreements but nothing big. We've got to keep it that way forever. I know that there will be lot of times that I will have to be more tolerant than I am now. After I get back from overseas, for a while, it's going to be hard for me to get along with anyone. I hope you'll realize that fact.

We think we know each other pretty well, but, actually, we have a lot to learn about each other. Little things that you do will probably get on my nerves at times and vice versa. I know that our love will overcome them if we give it half a chance. Darling, I'm not trying to give a lecture on how to make marriage a success, but merely mentioning these things in order that nothing possible can go wrong with our happiness. I know that we can be happy together, as happy as any two people in the world can be. We've proven that time and time again, and we'll keep right on proving it. Darling, you may think I sound silly, and I probably do, but I mean every word I write on this paper.

Mail sure has been slow for the last two weeks. I got 2 letters this week and no more. One was from you and one was from Dad. We think it will come in better from now on. At least we hope so. Mail sure means a lot to the boys over here. If they get mail regularly everything's O.K., but if they don't, they're pretty hard to get along with.

Goodnight, Darling, and sweet dreams.

All My Love for You,

Bob

---·--/ -···-/·-·/·-··/··/-·/--·/

September 30, 1944

My Darling Frances,

I got my pictures back today, and I'm going to send you one tonight. I may send it in a separate envelope. I think it's pretty good. It flatters me a hell of a lot. I hope you like the picture. I got two letters from you today!

All My Love for You,

Bob

---·--/ -···-/·-·/·-··/··/-·/--·/

October 5, 1944

My Darling Frances,

I'm so tired and sleepy tonight that I don't know if I'll get to finish this letter or not. I suppose by the time you receive this letter you have thought that I have completely forgotten you, but, Darling, you know I haven't. I try to write as often as I can, but sometimes it's impossible.

Darling, don't let anyone ever tell you war isn't hell, because it is. It's hard to conceive there is a war on till you go on a mission, then there is no doubt about it. We can buy cigarettes over here for $.40 a carton alright, but they are rationed and we are lucky if we get a pack a week.

You wanted to know what the Presidential Citation was for, well it was for a mission over an oil refinery at Ploesti, Romania. The Allies now have it in their control. I had a day off and, we went to town and saw a lousy show, "Rosie the Riveter," or something like that.

I haven't received the books or stationery as yet, but it takes quite a while for packages to get here. I hope I have time to read the books when I do get them. I should have more time to read though as winter is coming on, and naturally, it will slow our flying down.

I got a letter from Dad today. It was very short. At the end he said it was just a report on the Bulldog [New Albany High School] football game and not a letter. Ha! He went to the game and sat next to Bill and Agatha. He said Agatha kept him pretty busy talking. Can you imagine that?

Goodnight, Darling, and sweet dreams.

All My Love for My Wife,

Bob

---·--/ -···-/·-·/·-··/··/-·/--·/

The constant bombing runs took their toll on the bomber crews mentally and physically. When Bob was flying combat missions over enemy territory in 1944, the crew members had a one-in-three chance of returning safely home. The bomber crews who had a few missions under their belts felt the emotional stress. The complete helplessness of flying through flak and being attacked by enemy planes created a terrible anxiety. When on the ground, the crew members were described as "quiet, edgy, and morose."

Bob seldom wrote home about his fears or his anxieties about flying missions. He never fully articulated seeing other B-17s go down or close calls to his own plane. Overall, his letters were positive and optimistic. Only a few obtuse comments about his state of mind and his fears appeared in his letters home.

Bob was often asked if he had ever been scared during the war. His answer was always, "Yes, all the time. We were all scared." There were only three possible outcomes of every mission. You parachuted out of a doomed aircraft to imprisonment, or worse, you died, or you returned safely.

War correspondent Ernie Pyle described battle fatigue simply and eloquently, "They had found more war than the human spirit can endure."

Chapter Eleven

That Flak Is Mean

> "...the greater courage was exercised by the men not while they were airborne, but rather when they made the decision to climb aboard their aircraft before each and every sortie. This was especially true given the fact that every one of them was a volunteer."

A Typical Bombing Mission Day for Bob

On a typical day that involved flying a mission, crews were awakened around 4 A.M. They dressed and went to breakfast. After breakfast, they climbed into a 6x6 truck and traveled about a mile to group headquarters. At the headquarters, all the crews of the 97th Bombardment Group attended a briefing session. The crews were told what target they were to bomb as well as what to expect from the enemy, including the number of anti-aircraft guns near the target and the number of enemy fighter planes in the target area, plus other pertinent information.

After the general briefing, Bob would attend a radio operator's briefing where he and other radio operators would receive a canvas packet containing the code card for the day and the radio frequencies to be used. It was the radio operator's responsibility to memorize the code of the day, an important password needed to send and receive messages. When requested by the pilot, he would also obtain weather reports. "Pilots, navigators, and bombardiers would also receive an information Signals sheet, so that before climbing into a B-17, they would know call signs, code words, VHF channels, fighter call signs, and answering call signs." The crews would then go to the parachute shack, pick up their parachutes, and then proceed to the airfield. At the airfield, they would get their .50-caliber guns and ammunition.

On more than one occasion a bomb load would be changed at the last minute with a different type or number of bombs. At first, it struck Bob as odd that the bombs coming out of the plane's bomb bay would simply be dropped onto a stand on the taxiway. Sometimes, it seemed, haphazardly, but the bombs were not yet armed. The bombs were armed with a wire that ran through a propeller at the back of the bomb and attached to the airplane. When the bombs dropped, the wire disengaged from the bomb propeller, which immediately began spinning. After so many propeller revolutions, the bomb was armed.

Bob and his crew would take off at approximately 9 a.m., join the formation, and head out toward the target. As soon as they gained some altitude, the crew would test-fire all thirteen machine guns. At 10,000 feet, they put on their oxygen masks, as the B-17 did not have a pressurized cabin like the airplanes of today. The pilot would call for an oxygen check about every fifteen minutes. All the crew members would reply in a predetermined order.

Joining the large formation of bombers on their way to the target of the day was the fighter escort. In Bob's case, the fighter escort was composed of P-51 Mustang fighter planes. It would take three to four hours or more to reach the target. To break the monotony, Bob would ask the pilot for permission to tune into the Armed Forces Network so that the crew could listen to music and news over the intercom. While listening to the radio, all the gunners kept their eyes open for enemy fighter planes.

After flying for several hours, the bomber formation approached the target. If they were lucky, the crew reached the Initial Point (IP) without being attacked by enemy fighter planes. From the IP to the target, (approximately 40 miles from the target) the bomber group had to fly straight and at the same altitude until the bombs were dropped, making them most vulnerable to flak. "The main goal was to stay in formation. A tight formation was needed to fend off the fighters, and it made a better bomb pattern. Most of our bomb patterns were diamond shaped. We dropped all sorts of different bombs," Bob said.

After the bombs were dropped by the B-17s, they would make a sharp 90-degree downturn to escape the heavy flak. The missions were sometimes too far away for the B-17s to easily return to their base. It wasn't unusual for the planes to return with their engines running on fumes, the fuel gauge on empty. To counter this, crews on the return trip would often drop the plane's ball turret, which was very heavy, as well as ammunition and even machine guns, allowing for a few more miles of fuel efficiency.

"Sometimes you would get disoriented during or after a bombing run, and a couple of times the whole squadron broke up. Then you'd have to go back with just one or two planes. After you got off the target and amidst the chaos, the formation just disappeared. It was hectic. Some of the planes were hit, and they'd pull off. One time the whole group just broke up; we couldn't stay together. Two other airplanes joined up with us and we went back with three airplanes," Bob recalled.

Landing back at their base and before the flight crew was able to exit the aircraft, the mechanics began patching the flak holes in the aluminum covering. Bombers often had 200 to 300 flak holes. After exiting the airplane and making their way to Group Headquarters, crews were greeted by two Red Cross women who gave them coffee and donuts. The Army gave each crew member a shot of bourbon. Some would save their shots and trade them for cigarettes.

Crew members were then debriefed, relating all the happenings of the mission to the debriefing officers. Afterwards, they were allowed to return to their squadron area, eat dinner, and retire to their tents for the night, ending a typical mission day.

Bob remarked, "It didn't really get easier as you flew one mission after another. Where I was stationed in Foggia, Italy, you had to fly 50 missions before you got to go home, and the closer you get to that, the harder it is."

Some of Bob's B-17 Missions

There are two main uses for heavy bombers in war. Strategic bombing, as defined by the Air Force, "...strikes at the economy, it attempts to cripple its war potential by blows at industrial production, civilian morale, and communications. Tactical bombardment is immediate support of movements of air, land, or sea forces." During WWII, the B-17 bomber was used in both strategic and tactical missions.

Bob said, "Our first mission was an easy mission. We flew out to blow up a bridge in southern France. The Allied forces were getting ready for the invasion of southern France, which of course we didn't know about at the time. After that mission I thought this was going to be a snap. We didn't have any problems at all." That would soon change. On subsequent missions, "You'd come upon the target, and it was so black you'd swear it was a cloud, but that's the burst from the shells, the flak."

"A couple of missions we flew were tactical missions, where we were helping the ground forces. One was over Bologna, Italy, bombing enemy troops there. Another was over Athens, Greece. The Germans were getting out of Greece, and we caught them out in the open, no flak or anything. We came out over the water and plastered them. That was an easy mission."

Most of the missions for Bob and his crew were strategic ones, mainly bombing oil refineries, marshalling yards, and munition factories. One device the Allies started to use in bombing railroad marshalling yards was to drop delayed bombs. By using forced laborers from territories that the Nazis had conquered and men from concentration camps, the Germans could quickly get a bombed-out railroad marshalling yard back to functioning within twelve hours, with the German trains running on schedule again. To compensate, the Allies began dropping delayed bombs on the marshalling yards. Delayed bombs did not go off at impact. They were set to go off later, making it more difficult to rebuild railroad hubs.

Bob recalled, "The two hardest missions were Ploiesti, Romania, and Munich, Germany. I flew over each of those twice. They really tried to guard their oil refineries. In Ploiesti, they had a circle around the city with about five refineries, one right in the middle of the city. On the second mission I flew there, the Germans had put up smokescreens. They knew we were coming. They tried to cover and hide the target. A P-38 Lightning was sent out ahead of us, and he radioed back and told us which target was open. We were briefed on all the targets and ours happened to be the one in the middle of the city. The problem was that the Germans had their anti-aircraft guns circling the city, so you get in there once facing fire, then get more fire on your way out going the other way. That flak is mean. Flak brought down more planes than fighters ever did."

Bob continued, "There were a few times we saw air combat amongst the fighters, but not many. We were flying so late in the war that the German air force was almost gone. All they had was that 262 jet. We got hit by enemy aircraft one time that I remember. That's a funny story. When we got back, as always, we were debriefed. An officer asked me how many rounds I'd fired from my .50-caliber, and I said, 'How many rounds does it hold? I shot 'em all.'"

On one bombing run, shrapnel from exploding flak that had pierced through the plane's thin aluminum skin hit the left side of Bob's hand. This earned his Purple Heart, although initially he wasn't going to apply for it. Then he learned that points were awarded for getting out of the service if a person got the medal. "I'm not too proud of that medal," Bob joked, "but it got me home quicker."

While stationed near Foggia, Italy, Bob flew missions to Ploiesti, Romania; Blechhammer, Lechfeld, and Munich, Germany; Vienna and Wiener Neustadt, Austria; Athens, Greece; Oswiecim, Poland; Pardubice, Czechoslovakia [now Czech Republic]; and the invasion of southern France. The crew also flew to various targets in Bulgaria and Hungary.

−−−·−−/ −···−/·−·/·−··/··/−·/−−·/

October 9, 1944

My Darling Frances,

We had another day off today, and we accomplished quite a bit. We finished the stove for our tent that we had been working on for the last 2 weeks. We have it going now, and it sure keeps the tent nice and warm. Maybe I won't freeze after all. I imagine the people back home wouldn't exactly appreciate the fact that we are using good gasoline for fuel, but who cares.

The most wonderful thing happened today, but I can't tell you about it. Believe me when I say God does answer prayers. There are still lots of good things that happen in this war-torn world.

You were telling me about the mouse you had in your bedroom, well we now have about 5 in our tent. Last night one of them ran across the foot of my cot. We already have a counterattack planned for tonight. Leonard's wife sent him a mouse trap, and we have it set for the kill.

Darling, I have to put in 50 missions before I can come home. I think you asked me about that. Sometimes a mission counts 2 if we have to go a long way. I now have 23 missions. I now have the Air Medal and one Oak Leaf Cluster on it. I, also, have 3 stars on my European Theater ribbon. One is for the Italian Campaign, one for the air battle, and one for the invasion of southern France. That is the extent of my ribbons. I don't know if the folks know how many missions I have flown. I'll let them know when I get to 50. It's OK you telling Mother about the citation. I guess I forgot to tell her. Oh yes, that's another ribbon. I can wear a citation ribbon. I'd about forgotten about that one.

I live for the day, Darling, that I can slip another ring on the same finger, and I don't think it will be too much longer. I love my future wife very much, and I wish I had her in my arms this very moment.

With All My Love for You Alone,

Bob

---·--/ -···-/·-·/·-··/··/-·/--·/

The Distinguished Unit Citation award is given to units of the uniformed services of the US, and those of allied countries for extraordinary heroism in action against an armed enemy on or after December 7, 1941. Bob was awarded the Unit Citation for two raids over Ploiesti, Romania. He was awarded medals for his participation in the Italian campaign, the air battle and the invasion of southern France, with three stars. He received the Air Medal with one Oak Leaf Cluster for his combat missions over enemy territory. He earned the Purple Heart Medal for the flak wound to his hand.

---·--/ -···-/·-·/·-··/··/-·/--·/

October 15, 1944

My Darling Frances,

I sure like what you did first in that letter today. That's exactly what we will do first. How do you like that? I'm going to be an uncle in

April, and I'm not even married yet, but I will be when April comes around.

Darling, I now have 26 missions as of today, and I have to fly 50, no more, just 50. But let me tell you 50 is enough.

Darling, it sure will be a happy day when I don't have to write to you anymore, but I can talk to you in person and then if that's not good enough I can take you in my arms and show you what I mean.

I'm getting sleepy and I have to get up early tomorrow, so I'm afraid this is all for now. Goodnight, Darling, and sweet dreams.

All My Love, Darling, for You,

Bob

P.S. I'm sending you a kiss C.O.D. (Cash on Delivery)

---.--/ -...-/.-./.-../../-./--./

In late 1943, the life expectancy of a B-17 crewman was eleven missions before being shot down or captured. Twenty-five was initially the number of missions required to complete a tour of duty. When Bob was training with his crew in the United States in 1944, they estimated completing 25 missions and being home by Christmas. By the time Bob made it to Foggia, Italy, the required number of missions had gone up to 50.

---.--/ -...-/.-./.-../../-./--./

October 20, 1944

My Darling Frances,

No mail today but I didn't really expect any as I got one from Sis and one from your mother yesterday. Sis said you and your mother were over home the other day and also that her and Helen were the only ones home. I guess she and Helen entertained you successfully.

It's kind of chilly out tonight, but we have our stove going tonight and it's really cozy here in the tent, but I can think of another place I'd rather be.

We caught a mouse last night, and we're out to get another one tonight. They've been running up and down the top of our beds for the last three nights, and we're trying to put a stop to it by catching all of them, but it looks like it's going to be a pretty big order.

I'm halfway through but I don't know whether I can stand being away from you that much longer or not, but I guess I'll live through it even though it is quite an ordeal. I sure miss you, Darling, and I can't get back to you too soon. We're going to have a marvelous time, Darling, and I'm living only for that day.

All My Love, Darling, for You Alone,

Bob

–––·––/ –···–/·–·/·–··/··/–·/––·/

This would be Bob's last letter to Frances before his plane was shot down.

On October 23, 1944, while flying on their 32nd mission, over Skoda Works in Pilsen, Czechoslovakia [now Czech Republic], Bob's aircraft suffered severe damage from flak anti-aircraft guns. As the flak rocked the plane, Bob got out of his seat in the radio room and sat on a tin box mounted on the floor in the center of the plane, creating a small "safe space," or at least "safer" space, that reduced the likelihood of being hit with flak. Minimize your space and minimize the potential damage. Then, a piece of flak penetrated the plane, into the radio room through the radio operator's seat, "rattling around in there," as Bob noted, which caused him to get down on his hands and knees to find the piece of flak. Had he still been seated at the radio he'd have been killed. Another lucky break that was critical to Bob's survival came when the pilot ordered the crew over the intercom to "bail out," meaning parachute out of the plane.

"We were an alternate crew that day," Bob said. "We weren't even supposed to fly that day. It was our day off. They had another crew that had a taxiing accident that damaged two planes, so we had to fly a spare. We were called back in. We had a modified B-17F model with a chin turret, and we ended up going over the target by ourselves, which is probably why we got shot down. When you're over the target area, the pilots would throttle it all the way. We couldn't keep up with the others. But we all got out, all of ten of us got out."

When a wounded B-17 started to go down, it usually went into a spin. At that point the crew was trapped by centrifugal force and could not escape. Bob credits his pilot with getting the whole crew out before the plane went into a spin. Rarely were ten parachutes safely released from a falling B-17 aircraft.

A delayed parachute jump was required, due to the altitude of the aircraft, necessitating a freefall to below 15,000 feet. Opening one's parachute above this altitude would leave the jumper floating with little or no oxygen, resulting in death. Parachutes were not always worn during the actual flight time. "The parachutes themselves were placed near every crew station, although some men did not know how to use them properly, and no one on board had ever jumped out of an airplane. That had not been part of their training."

The right waist gunner jumped out of the open bomb-bay ahead of Bob, and when the gunner pulled the cord and opened his chute Bob was above him. Bob pulled the cord and his chute opened with a hard jerk. Everything seemed alright until Bob passed by the waist gunner as if he were stationary in the sky. Bob was sure his chute had opened because it had jerked him so hard, but he knew he was in some sort of trouble. He was dropping too fast. Looking up, Bob discovered he had a "Mae West" chute, a parachute malfunction with two blossoms instead of one. He was later told by a veteran paratrooper that he could have grabbed a shroud line, and spilled that chute, letting it reopen without the two blossoms. But Bob knew there was no way he would have spilled that chute for fear of it not opening again. Bob said, "Under other circumstances I might have enjoyed my descent to earth, as it is very quiet and peaceful drifting down to earth in a parachute."

The ground was completely covered with clouds. Bob passed through clouds that he assumed were several thousand feet above ground. His assumption was wrong, as he planted hard into the earth in a small cornfield in hilly terrain. With the chute descending faster than normal, he was fortunate to have landed in a muddy field. He was also completely relaxed, resulting in only an injury to his ankle. This was another lucky break for Bob. If he had landed on any other surface his injuries could have been life threatening. The corn in his landing field had been harvested and stacked, so he hid the parachute under one of the corn stacks. The main problem now was the footprints he left in the muddy field, which pointed to the hidden parachute. Escaping capture became the priority, but that was impossible unless a friendly inhabitant offered help.

The Air Force furnished crews with an escape kit, consisting of $50 in American currency, a compass, silk maps of Europe, a water purification kit, and a chocolate bar. Bob was faced with a monumental task. The nearest Allied territory was more than 500 miles from Pilsen. He managed to escape detection for a day and a half by moving late in the afternoon from one wooded area to another wooded area.

On the second day, as he was attempting to cross a field to a wooded area, a farmer came out of another wooded area. G-2 Army intelligence recommended getting help to escape, preferably from common people like farmers. Keeping this in mind, Bob helped the farmer herd his cattle into a small village, although Bob could not speak German. After entering the village, Bob was immediately surrounded by approximately 50 villagers and accosted by an elderly man with a German Walther P38 pistol in hand.

The man wasted no time sticking the pistol in Bob's stomach and yelling at him in German. Then it dawned on Bob that the man wanted him to surrender his weapon, which he didn't have. Bob finally convinced him by hand signals that he had no weapon, at which time the man put his pistol away, and Bob could breathe a sigh of relief. Bob later recalled this was one of the scariest moments of his military experience. The old man's finger was on the trigger, and the man was shaking so hard Bob feared the gun might go off. The elderly man and a few people escorted Bob to a house. When he entered, the first things he saw were a Nazi swastika and a picture of Hitler hanging on the wall. "That's when I knew I'd had it," Bob recounted. One of the reasons he received no help from the locals was the site where he landed. It was an area of Czechoslovakia called the Sudetenland, which had belonged to Germany prior to World War I. The people Bob hoped to receive help from were Germans.

This moment was more dangerous than Bob knew. Goebbels, Hitler's Propaganda Minister, had issued a kill-order to German civilians. This order encouraged German civilians to kill enemy fliers who had parachuted to safety in German territory. For downed flyers, getting into the hands of the Luftwaffe was their safest way to survive in enemy territory. The number of airmen who were brutally murdered by enemy civilians when they parachuted out of their doomed planes is unknown. Downed crewmen who escaped being attacked by enemy civilians on the ground would later confirm actual killings of airmen by civilians. All ten of Bob's crew survived their landings and were taken prisoner, which was extremely lucky.

Map showing Sudetenland with it's proximity to Germany

Chapter Twelve

The Telegram

My grandmother taught me to embroider and quilt when I was a little girl. We would sit and do our needlework and enjoy each other's company. As kids tend to do, I was asking her questions one day while doing our needlework. The instant I asked the question, I knew I shouldn't have. I wanted to take it back, but it couldn't be taken back.

"Grandma, what was the worst day of your life?"

Her eyes immediately filled with tears, and her countenance had a stark look of fear and sorrow. Sixty years later, I can still see that look on her face. I felt so terrible seeing her cry, that tears rolled down my face, too. It was not just her face, but her whole body that was affected. She took a deep breath and waited a minute before she answered. I didn't think she wanted to answer, but she did.

"The worst day of my life was the day the telegram came. The one that said Bobby had been shot down and was missing in action," she answered.

I didn't completely understand what she meant, but I knew better than to ask for clarification. It was a crushing moment. I was sure she would never ask me to her house again. I learned many years later that when the telegram came my grandmother mentally and physically collapsed. She was bedridden and unable to function for several weeks.

How many families received a telegram like that? The death toll of personnel killed or missing in action in combat in WWII was over 400,000. On the Freedom Wall at the WWII Memorial in Washington, D.C., there are 4,048 gold stars. Each star represents 100 American military deaths and MIAs. It's a powerful image that puts the cost of war in a visual form that helps us to grasp the enormity of the sacrifice.

How did it affect the town of New Albany? Ninety-eight men from New Albany were killed in action. Many others were wounded. How did it effect Bob and Frances' crew of friends? One of Frances' closest girlfriends lost her fiancé, and there were others they knew. Friends, acquaintances, and neighbors were wounded, missing in action, or they paid the ultimate price. And now Bob was missing in action over enemy territory.

Bob was shot down on October 23, 1944. His family was notified a few days later via telegram that he was missing in action. No further information on his survival was provided. A newspaper article from the *New Albany Tribune,* dated November 9, 1944, states that the family had received no further news. Later in November, the family received two official letters from the Army Air Force giving more details. The letters stated that Bob's plane had been shot down and destroyed with no update on his whereabouts.

The moment when Bob's family and Frances first learned that he was alive and imprisoned in a prisoner-of-war camp is unknown. How long did they wait to hear of Bob's fate? The mothers and fathers of Bob's crew members corresponded with each other. One story is that a fellow crew member had seen Bob alive and wrote telling his mother, and his mother wrote to alert Bob's mother. Regardless of how and when the news reached home, it was an anxious few months until they knew for certain that Bob was alive.

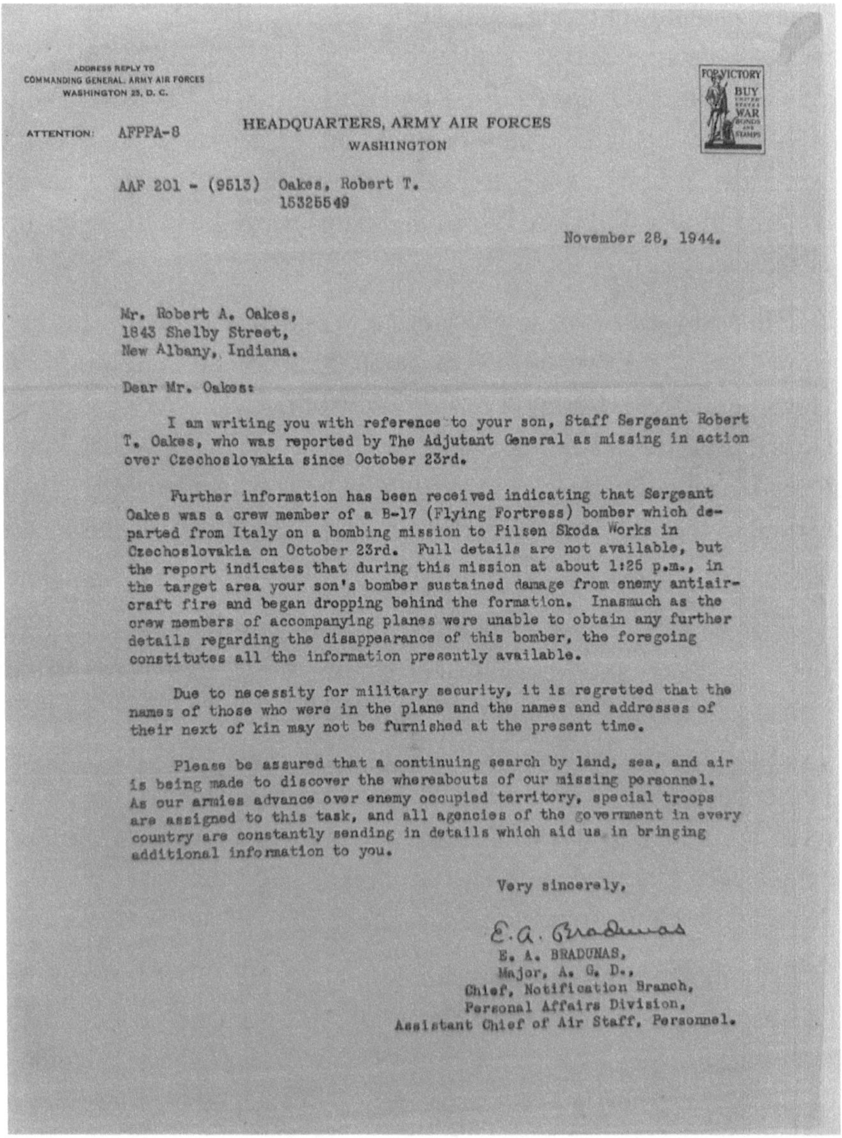

ADDRESS REPLY TO
COMMANDING GENERAL, ARMY AIR FORCES
WASHINGTON 25, D. C.

FOR VICTORY BUY UNITED STATES WAR BONDS AND STAMPS

ATTENTION: AFPPA-8

HEADQUARTERS, ARMY AIR FORCES
WASHINGTON

AAF 201 - (9513) Oakes, Robert T.
15325549

November 28, 1944.

Mr. Robert A. Oakes,
1843 Shelby Street,
New Albany, Indiana.

Dear Mr. Oakes:

I am writing you with reference to your son, Staff Sergeant Robert T. Oakes, who was reported by The Adjutant General as missing in action over Czechoslovakia since October 23rd.

Further information has been received indicating that Sergeant Oakes was a crew member of a B-17 (Flying Fortress) bomber which departed from Italy on a bombing mission to Pilsen Skoda Works in Czechoslovakia on October 23rd. Full details are not available, but the report indicates that during this mission at about 1:25 p.m., in the target area your son's bomber sustained damage from enemy antiaircraft fire and began dropping behind the formation. Inasmuch as the crew members of accompanying planes were unable to obtain any further details regarding the disappearance of this bomber, the foregoing constitutes all the information presently available.

Due to necessity for military security, it is regretted that the names of those who were in the plane and the names and addresses of their next of kin may not be furnished at the present time.

Please be assured that a continuing search by land, sea, and air is being made to discover the whereabouts of our missing personnel. As our armies advance over enemy occupied territory, special troops are assigned to this task, and all agencies of the government in every country are constantly sending in details which aid us in bringing additional information to you.

Very sincerely,

E. A. Bradunas

E. A. BRADUNAS,
Major, A. G. D.,
Chief, Notification Branch,
Personal Affairs Division,
Assistant Chief of Air Staff, Personnel.

Official letter sent to Oakes famiy on November 28, 1944

The definitive news that Bob was alive came from him. He was allowed to write two postcards. One came to his family, dated November 19, 1944, and one came to Frances, dated December 5, 1944. How long it took from the dates they were mailed until the postcards were delivered is unknown, but he was alive! He was in enemy hands, but he was alive! One can only imagine the happiness and relief that came from these two postcards.

They did not know the details of Bob's ordeal, but they knew him. If he could survive, he would. He was made of strong fiber, fortified with his faith, his family, and his love for Frances. He would come home.

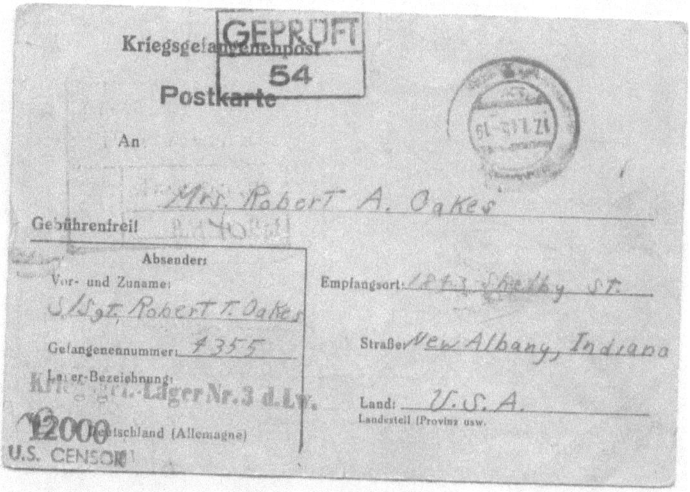

Kriegsgefangenenpost
GEPRÜFT 54
Postkarte

An Mrs. Robert A. Oakes

Gebührenfrei!

Absender:
Vor- und Zuname: S/Sgt. Robert T. Oakes
Gefangenennummer: #355
Lager-Bezeichnung: Kriegsgef.-Lager Nr. 3 d. Lw.
Deutschland (Allemagne)

Empfangsort: 1823 Shelby St.
Straße: New Albany, Indiana
Land: U. S. A.
Landesteil (Provinz usw.

12000
U.S. CENSOR

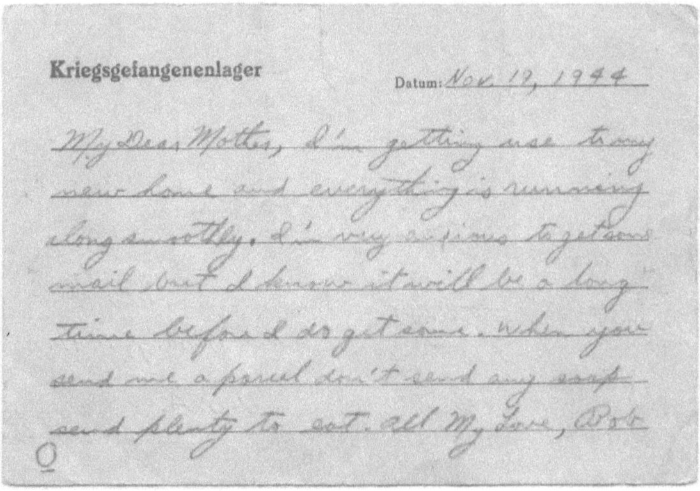

Kriegsgefangenenlager

Datum: Nov. 19, 1944

My Dear Mother, I'm getting use to my new home and everything is running along smoothly. I'm very anxious to get some mail but I know it will be a long time before I do get some. When you send me a parcel don't send any soap send plenty to eat. All My Love, Bob

Postcard from Bob to his parents from the P.O.W. camp in Poland.

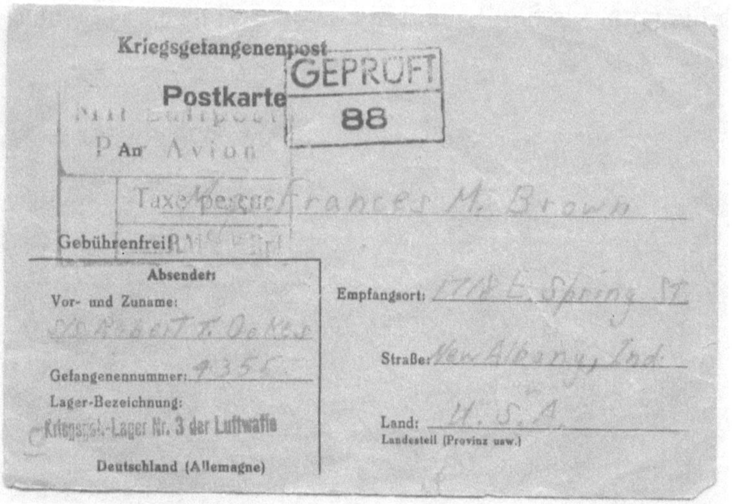
Kriegsgefangenenpost
Postkarte
GEPRÜFT
88
Mit Luftpost
Par Avion
An
Taxe perçue
Frances M. Brown
Gebührenfrei
Absender:
Vor- und Zuname: Sgt Robert F. Oakes
Gefangenennummer: 9356
Lager-Bezeichnung:
Kriegsgef.-Lager Nr. 3 der Luftwaffe
Deutschland (Allemagne)
Empfangsort: 1718 E. Spring St
Straße: New Albany, Ind.
Land: U. S. A.
Landesteil (Provinz usw.)

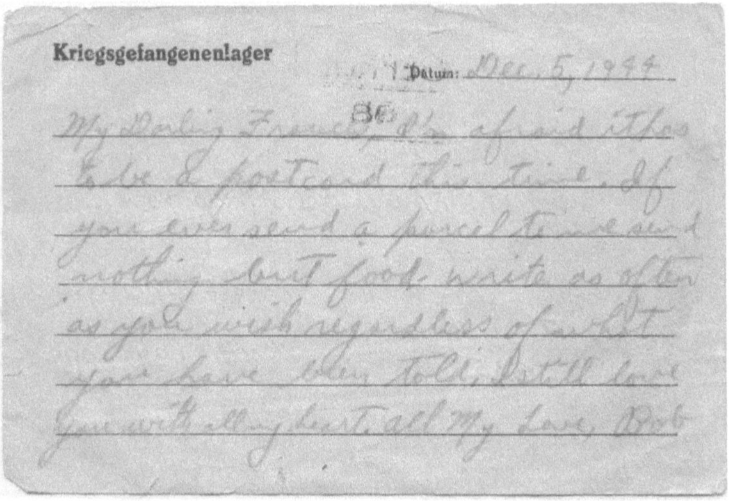
Kriegsgefangenenlager
Datum: Dec. 5, 1944
88
My Darling Frances, I'm afraid it has to be a postcard this time. If you ever send a parcel to me send nothing but food. write as often as you wish regardless of what you have been told, I still love you with all my heart. all My Love, Bob

Postcard from Bob to Frances from the P.O.W. camp in Poland.

Chapter Thirteen

POW #4355

> "Our airmen who were prisoners of the Germans are special. They were there, in the belly of the beast. They saw and experienced the tyranny that other airmen knew only from afar."
>
> —*Lieutenant Colonel Robert "Rosie" Rosenthal,*
> *100th Bombardment Group*

Bob spent his first night in enemy territory in a basement cell in a small village jail. The cell was cold and damp, and he slept very little. He was transferred the next day to a Luftwaffe base in the city of Eger [now Cheb, Czech Republic], located on the Germany-Czechoslovakia border. He soon discovered that Richard Leonard, his B-17's tail gunner, was being held at the same base.

The next morning, Bob and Richard boarded a train escorted by two Luftwaffe guards for the journey to Frankfurt, Germany, to be interrogated. It was a frightening trip, as it was to a place where some prisoners did not return. While they were being escorted through the streets of Eger to the railroad station, some civilians started to yell and throw rocks at them. This prompted the guards to draw their weapons and restrain the locals from harming the prisoners. The anger was justified, as their town had recently been hit by Allied bombers.

At this time both Bob and Richard were smokers, and they didn't have any cigarettes. The guards smoked, but they rolled their own, so they gave Bob and Richard paper and tobacco to roll their own cigarettes. The prisoners made a mess of it, so the guards rolled them two, proclaiming Bob and Richard as "dummkopf Amerikaners."

Cursed and threatened by the locals, scoffed at by their guards, frightened by what may await them, an unexpected act of kindness appeared. On the train, a woman sitting behind them gave Bob and Richard apples to eat. This was an act of bravery done in defiance of the guards and the others on the train. The gesture had a profound effect on Bob. It was a turning point for him during those trying times. There was goodness in this horrible situation. Perhaps, things were going to be okay. A small act of goodwill appeared at the darkest time, when he needed it the most.

Interrogation

From the bomb-damaged Frankfurt railroad station, the prisoners were taken via streetcar to the Luftwaffe interrogation center in Oberursel, a suburb of Frankfurt. This was the Dulag Luft [Durchgangslager der Luftwaffe], a transit camp where captured members of the United States Army Air Force were collected and questioned. The conditions were grim. It was a dark, moldy, and horribly smelling place full of rats and fleas. During interrogation, prisoners were queried about everything. They questioned Bob about nationality, family and relatives, civilian occupation, army background, equipment, bases, technology, and seemingly irrelevant matters. Bob was relieved because he did not know much of anything.

This was normal, as only officers were privy to important intelligence. To Bob, it seemed that the Germans were most interested in finding out what he knew about an advanced radar technology purportedly housed in the wings of Allied aircraft. Again, Bob had no knowledge of such technology. Yet, the Germans already knew a great deal about him. They knew where he was from, knew about his family, and other personal information. He wondered, "How do they know so much about my family in Indiana?" And now they were trying to use that against him.

When they were not being interrogated, prisoners were kept in solitary confinement. "You cannot know how your mind can be altered, and your morale destroyed when you are in solitary confinement," Bob later noted. In addition to no food, the solitary confinement cell was extremely cold. The heater control was on the corridor wall, and when a POW had to use the bathroom, he tripped a signal that alerted the guard, who came and escorted him to the toilet. On the way to the toilet, Bob would turn the heat on, and it would stay on until the guard discovered it and turned it off.

Other prisoners echoed Bob's experience. Charles G. Janis, a former POW, wrote of his experience in the Luftwaffe interrogation center. "I believe, that of all Prisoner of War phases, this stay at Frankfurt was, by far, the most harrowing. The conditions were most unpleasant; the food and lodging were the worst possible and the menacing attitude of the guards greatly contributed to the mental unrest of the prisoner. Most unnerving, however, was the suspense before the actual questioning."

On the third day of Bob's interrogation, the interrogator, a "nasty" German colonel who spoke excellent English, asked where Bob's gas mask was. Bob told him that he had left it back in Italy. The colonel said not to worry, as he had also left his mask in Italy when the Germans had retreated out of southern Italy. He then told Bob that his interrogation was over.

Stalag Luft P.O.W. guard tower, "no man's land", and barbed wire fences.

After his interrogation, Bob was transported in a railroad boxcar to another transit camp at Wetzlar,

Germany. From Wetzlar, Bob and some 50 other POWs were again transported in boxcars, this time to the Stalag Luft IV prison camp in Gross Tychow, Pomerania, now Tychowo, Poland.

Stalag Luft IV

Stalag Luft IV was divided into four areas, or camps, called lagers. The lagers were separated by two rows of barbed-wire fencing, with a "no man's land" between the fences. Located on the perimeter of each lager were guard towers spaced at 100-foot intervals. Located ten feet from the fences was a warning wire about three feet high. If you crossed the wire, the guards would shoot you.

Opened in the summer of 1944, Stalag Luft IV was designed to hold 1,600 prisoners in each lager, but it soon held from 2,300 to 2,500 prisoners in each area. Bob was assigned to a barracks that was so overcrowded that his makeshift bed was under a table on the wooden floor in the middle of the room. It was a mat filled with what felt like old paper for padding. Bunks for the other prisoners were stacked three beds high.

Each morning the prisoners were roused from sleep at an early hour to fall in formation in front of the barracks for roll call. Someone would usually fail to make roll call, and the POWs would be forced to spend more time in the bitter cold while the German guards woke the late sleeper and removed him from the barracks. If the count was off, then the guards had to start all over again. Bob soon learned how to count in German.

Sometime later, daily rations of food would be distributed. This usually consisted of a half-cup of potatoes, a piece of bread equivalent to about one-seventh of a small loaf, jam, and coffee. One of the main bread ingredients was sawdust. Bob recalled, "The bread and coffee tasted terrible, but after consistently eating it and still literally starving, it was palatable enough." In the beginning of Bob's captivity, horse meat would be served on occasion, but for the last three months of captivity the POWs ate no meat. The food was always cold and horrible tasting, and there was just enough to keep a man alive.

Roger Armstrong, a B-17 radio operator who was in the same POW barracks as Bob, wrote in his book *USA The Hard Way*: "The big event was when the Germans announced there would be barley cereal...Barley cereal meant we could possibly have two small meals on the same day. When we actually received the cereal, it would be dished up, and we tried to eat it slowly so it would last longer. It usually contained weevils (small beetles), but if you didn't look too close it didn't seem to bother any of us."

The Red Cross sent parcels of food weekly (logistically weekly deliveries were not always possible) to prisoners in every POW camp until the end of the war. Whether the prisoners received their package or not was uncertain, as the Germans sometimes hoarded the Red Cross parcels intended for the POWs, using the rations to feed themselves. This happened in the camp Bob was in.

Red Cross Package Contents received by an Army airman held prisoner in Stalag Luft 1.
(Contents varied throughout the war)

- 1 lb can of powdered milk
- 1 package of 10 assorted cookies
- 1 lb oleo margarine
- 8 oz cub sugar
- 8 oz Kraft cheese
- 6 oz biscuits
- 4 oz can of coffee
- 2 D-ration chocolate bars
- 6 oz can of jam or peanut butter
- 12 oz can of salmon or tuna
- 1 lb can of Spam
- 1 lb can of liver pate
- 1 lb raisins or prunes
- 5 packs of cigarettes
- 7 vitamin C tablets
- 12 oz vegetable soup concentrate

In one of the small notebooks that the prisoners had received from the YMCA, Bob covered pages with the names of the foods he would someday eat again. Of all the types of food he missed most, milk topped the list. (Bob's food list can be found in the glossary)

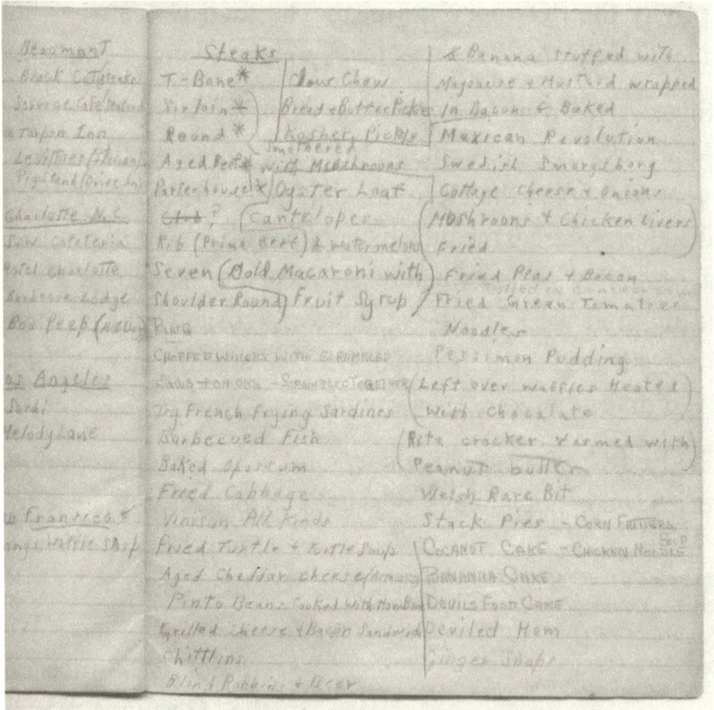

A page from Bob's POW notebook describing food he wanted to eat.

Between fantasizing about the food that you longed to eat, playing cards, reading a book, or walking around the lager with a buddy, the POWs managed to pass the time. Boredom had to be fought. There was a library in the camp, and books could be checked out, The prisoners also published a daily underground newspaper that was produced by someone listening to a hidden radio receiver getting the BBC news. The one-sheet newspaper was secretly read to a representative from each barracks, who then relayed the news to their roommates. During the time Bob was a POW, the Allied radio station was advising prisoners not to try to escape as the war was coming to an end.

One of the nicer German guards, who had worked at a hotel in New York before the war, would come into Bob's barracks and talk about anything but the war. He often wanted to talk about his time in the United States. He left New York because his workplace was not unionized, and returned to Germany where unions were popular. He would stand behind someone playing bridge and offer unwelcome advice on the game.

In a POW camp, there were men with a myriad of talents. Bob copied poems written by fellow prisoners that depicted their ordeals and their hopes for the future.

"Last Flight"

Big Birds filled with eggs of death
Darken the skies of day,
And the enemy's guns all blow their breath
To take her away.
Chicks were nestled beneath her wings
Each man with a job to do
Showing a courage known to kings
As their guns spit a mad tattoo.
Then through the path of the great bird's flight
A bullet has found her heart,
And slowed her down in her gallant flight
As she fought to do more than her part.
Then she cautioned her chicks to be ready
For her life was fading fast.
Her course was now unsteady
And, finally, she breathed her last.
Then each chick leaped from the great bird's wing
And then held with a trembling hand
That wonderful man-made silken thing
That carried them safely to land.
Now each chick had one thought in mind
That his time had come to die.
But he thought of the land he left behind
And offered a new kind of sigh.

—Author Unknown

"My Future with Her"

It's just a year or more ago
We said "So long," short and sweet you know.
She said she'd wait for me
No matter how long the war would be.
Soon the time will be for me to go home,
And I'll be like a king on a throne.
I'll have her always at my side
For then she'll be my own sweet bride.
We'll have a car, house, and a little ground
Just for two children to run around.
I know how happy we will be
Just us four, my wife, two kids, and me.
These are my future dreams you see,
That's the way I'd like it to be.
Things won't run smooth all the time.
I'll be happy with her love and she with mine.

—Wallace Edward, POW

Most medical problems were managed within the barracks, with the common physical complaints of the prisoners, besides starvation, being athlete's foot and lice. The lack of food contributed to rashes, swollen joints, maladies that proper diet would have cured. It certainly didn't help either that the POWs did not get to take showers. Medical staff and medical supplies were extremely limited.

Mail service to and from the POW camps was a primary concern to a prisoner. As quickly as possible, prisoners wanted to inform their families of their current situation. Many of the airmen POWs, including Bob, were originally listed as missing in action. The German system of notifying the proper authorities of the fate of an airman who parachuted out of a doomed airplane was not efficient or speedy. The Germans heavily censored letters sent from the POWs as well as letters coming in from the states. Bob only noted one time when he received a letter from home. His family and Frances each received only the one post card from Bob the whole time of his imprisonment.

After their hungry and boring days, the POWs were locked in their barracks at night. Then, the guards would turn loose several guard dogs in the compound in case anyone had any ideas of escaping.

The winter of 1944-45 was the coldest that Germany had experienced for 50 years. The temperature that winter averaged 10 to 15 degrees above zero. As with many other POWs, Bob slept with all his clothes on to keep warm. He would end up wearing the same clothes for seven and a half months. As the prisoners were slowly being starved, it became more difficult for them to fight off the cold.

The barracks had a removable ceiling, and the prisoners would remove the ceiling during the cold weather and tear off pieces of the wood truss above for firewood. There was a time when they feared they had removed too much structural wood, which might cause the roof to collapse. Fortunately, the roof survived.

The barracks were elevated about three feet above ground to prevent tunneling. One night after lockup, the POWs discovered that a guard was under the barracks trying to listen to their conversations. The prisoners spotted the exact location of the guard and dumped a bucket of cold water through the floor on top of him. After a string of German expletives, he managed to make a quick exit from under the barracks, much to the POWs delight.

Surprise inspections were also part of life in the camp. Guards would crash through the doors at any given hour during the day or night and rummage through prisoners' living spaces, looking for contraband or anything else deemed unacceptable, leaving sleeping quarters in disarray and the prisoners on edge. Finding a radio would result in serious punishment. Although Bob never saw it, he knew of the existence of at least one radio because they got news reports daily before the barracks were locked down at night. The Germans came over the intercom with their news, but it always ran about two weeks behind what was coming from the BBC.

"The guards had tunnel vision when it came to searching for things," Bob noted. "They had one thing on their minds and wouldn't see anything else. They'd come into a barracks, and they may be searching for a knife that we'd sharpened up. After they went through the first barracks, word would spread about what they were after, and we could hide that item, leaving other stuff out in the open. They would not do anything about the other stuff. That's how they operated."

Although Nazi Germany was a majority Protestant Christian nation, anti-church sentiment was strong among its leaders. Hitler openly persecuted religious leaders and those who disagreed with him. The POWs were men in desperate need of inspiration and comfort from religion. A few clergymen were allowed in POW camps to administer to the needs of the thousands interned there. The clergymen's mission to administer spiritual comfort and support was a constant hard-fought battle with the Germans. Despite the difficulties, religious services were conducted and well attended. Religious holidays were allowed to be celebrated, with Nazi guards posted to oversee the gatherings. There were also organized pageants and choral efforts to supplement the worship services. It was important for the POWs to place hopes and trust of a future deliverance in the hands of God. These men were first-hand witnesses to the death and destruction of war.

Flying missions over enemy territory had held horrific terrors, and now being a prisoner of war produced its own horrors. Charles G. Janis, who was a prisoner in the same camp at the same time as Bob, wrote of POWs as "these men who were alive but not living. Their wholehearted efforts to surmount the obstacles and abuse given them was more evidence that though a man's body may be held in bondage, his mind and heart are irretrievably his own."

Stalag Luft I

In February 1945, the POWs could hear Russian guns in the distance, so they knew the Russians were getting close. At this point in the war, there were approximately 10,000 prisoners in Stalag Luft IV. The Germans sent a British doctor around to ascertain the health of the prisoners, primarily to see if they could walk long distances. Due to his bad ankle that was injured when he parachuted out of his plane, plus his flat feet, Bob did not have to join the march. Instead, he and about 500 to 1,000 other POWs (from POW estimates) were loaded into crowded boxcars for a 200-mile, eleven-day trip to Stalag Luft I at Barth, Germany. Bob would later call his ankle injury "a lucky break."

A little known but terrible ordeal was inflicted on the POWs from across Germany and German-held countries during the last days of the war. To prevent the prisoners from being liberated by the advancing Russian armies the prisoners were forced to march all over Germany until the war ended. Many men died on these marches, although it is difficult to know exactly how many POWs perished on these forced marches. There are no official records, only the surviving POWs to tell the stories. This collection of marches goes by various names, but they are often referred to simply as The March.

By this point, the prisoners of war were in no shape for a forced march of up to thirteen miles a day. The Germans provided no food, water, or shelter, and the POWs often slept on the ground where they fell from exhaustion. To add to the misery, it was the coldest winter in fifty years. The POWs quickly ran out of any food they had managed to leave the camp with and found themselves deep in enemy territory, where the German population was also struggling to feed itself. The POWs had been part of the bombing campaign that had reduced towns in Germany to rubble. Traveling through towns they had helped bomb, there were not any friendly handouts from the locals, and sometimes the POWs were physically attacked. They marched until they reached another POW camp in Germany. A few of the POW marchers encountered Allied armies fighting their way into Germany.

It was not all roses for those spared from marching. Bob said that the eleven-day trip on the train were the most miserable days of his life. "We rode in boxcars that were so crowded that all of us could not lie down at the same time," Bob noted. "They provided two buckets to urinate in, but there was no facility for the number-two job." After about five days of travel, the guards informed the POWs that they would be allowed to visit the restroom at the next station. The prisoners wondered if the station's restroom would be large enough to service the whole train. They found out when they arrived. The guards herded the entire trainload of POWs to an empty field, which became the relief station. The temperature was well below freezing and not conductive to a successful outcome. "While all the prisoners strained with their pants down, with the cold wind blowing up our rear ends, a train of German women passed slowly by our not-so-private restroom," Bob remembered. "One of the prisoners declared that it was the largest 'mooning' to ever occur and would make the Guinness World Records."

Bob and the other POWs arrived at Stalag Luft I after their miserable train experience. The camp was on the Baltic Sea near Barth, Germany, a little over a hundred miles northwest of Berlin. Originally opened in 1941 as a British POW camp, the number of prisoners had substantially increased as the air war escalated. When Bob arrived, there were 7,717 American prisoners, 1,427 British prisoners along with some Canadian and Russian prisoners.

Continuing at the top of the list of miseries for the prisoners was the lack of food. The POWs experienced severe hunger in March and April 1945. The simple truth was that the Germans attempted to starve prisoners. The men in this camp were receiving only half of their Red Cross food parcels when Bob arrived. From the beginning of March 1945 until the end of the war in May 1945, the POWs received no Red Cross food parcels. Once a day they were served a piece of bread and one cup of watery stew. The stew contained no meat, and often consisted simply of potatoes and kohlrabi, a type of cabbage crop with a swollen stem. One day a stray cat made the mistake of wandering into their lager providing some of them with cat stew. Bob was one of the lucky POWs who feasted on cat that night. As Bob noted, "If you're hungry enough you'll eat anything. And we did." After the war, Bob carried a copy of the black bread recipe in his wallet as a reminder of what it felt like to truly starve.

Picture taken at Stalag Left I. Pictured left to right Eugene Anderson, Bob Oakes, and John Dawson.

Stalag Luft I had originally been a camp for British officers, so the accommodations were somewhat better than Stalag Luft IV. Bob was assigned room Number 9 of Barracks 303, with each barracks housing 24 men. The prisoners were issued two thin blankets, and they continued the practice of sleeping with all their clothing on to have some semblance of warmth. They were not given enough fuel to keep the small stove in their barracks producing adequate heat. The POWs had lost so much weight that this added to their inability to get warm.

Black Bread Recipe

Former prisoners of war of Nazi Germany may be interested in this recipe for WWII Black Bread. This recipe comes from the official record from the Food Providing Ministry published (top secret) Berlin 24.XI 1941 and the Director in Ministry Herr Mansfeld and Herr Moritz. It was agreed that the best mixture to bake black bread was:
50% bruised rye grain
20% sliced sugar beets
20% tree flour (saw dust)
10% minced leaves and straw
From our own experiences with the black bread, we also saw bits of glass and sand. Someone was cheating on the recipe!

— Joseph P. O'Donnell
20 O'Rourke Dr., Robbinsville, NJ 08691

Black bread recipe eaten daily by prisoners in POW camp.

On April 18, 1945, Bob received a letter. This was the only correspondence he received while held captive. It was a morale boost and gave him hope.

"Towards the end, the YMCA sent us things like musical instruments," Bob said. "We got a xylophone, and one of the prisoners could play it. So suddenly we had music in our room." Prisoners would barter and trade almost anything for cigarettes, but tea was top of mind for the British POWs. U.S. prisoners would receive tea in their Red Cross parcels, so the marketplace was open. Russian POWs were treated terribly and tasked with the most menial jobs in the camps, such as emptying the outdoor latrines. The horrible treatment of Soviet POWs by the Nazis included, starvation, forced labor, beatings, and murder. The Russian prisoners were considered subhuman by the Nazis and treated accordingly.

There were three hidden radios in Stalag Luft I that the Germans never found. Because of the news from the BBC broadcasts, POWs knew that the American and British were advancing into Germany from the west and that the Russians were advancing from the east.

American bombers flew over the camp in March. This was a happy incident that turned tragic. POWs were to lie face down in their barracks if Allied aircraft few over. Unfortunately, two POWs were in the latrine when the bombers flew over. As they tried to run to their barracks, they were shot and killed by the German guards.

Several weeks before the end of the war, the POWs found out that President Roosevelt had died on April 12, 1945. This was unsettling news for the prisoners, and their situation felt precarious. Roosevelt had been a constant, strong source of confidence and resolve. What would happen now?

Along with their many uncertainties, the prisoners did not know that it was Hitler's intention to exterminate all Allied prisoners. There were approximately 200,000 American, British, Canadian, French, and other Allied POWs and more than one million Russian POWs. Fortunately, most of Hitler's leaders opposed the plan, and it was not carried out.

Liberation

On April 30, at 11:20 p.m., the Germans abandoned the camp to avoid capture by the Russians. Through a crack in a door, Bob saw the guards scampering down from a guard tower. On the morning of May 1, 1945, the prisoners of Stalag Luft I awoke to no captors.

After the Germans abandoned the camp, the American and British POWs in Stalag Luft I sent out reconnaissance patrols to find the Russians and gain information. In addition to the Russians, the patrols found 51,000 American Red Cross packages stored in a warehouse nearby. Each POW received five Red Cross packages from that treasure trove. Keeping the Red Cross packages from the starving POWs was clearly an act of cruelty by the Germans in defiance of the Geneva Convention.

On May 2, around 10 p.m., a drunken and unruly Russian advance unit, still celebrating May Day, rolled up in tanks to the front gate of

Stalag Luft I to liberate the camp. This advance group of Russians was a disruptive force, randomly tearing down sections of the barbed wire fences and disrupting nearby Barth. Finally, the prisoners could walk freely about the camp, although they were still not officially allowed out.

Colonel Hubert Zemke, the Senior Allied Officer of Stalag Luft I, reportedly managed to keep the advance guards drunk for two days until the Russian general in charge of the northern Russian army arrived. The Russians wanted to march the whole camp to the Black Sea port of Odessa, a distance over 1,200 miles, where the POWs would be turned over to the United States authorities and shipped home. No doubt, this would be an impossible ordeal for thousands of starved prisoners. Zemke told the Russian general that he would not permit the march to Odessa. The Russians did not want to grant permission for flights over their air space, but after negotiations, the Russians allowed the United States Army Air Force to fly the POWs to safety in northern France. The key to negotiations was when the United States agreed to release a Russian general who had been captured by the Germans and then recaptured by United States troops.

Zemke was the former commander of the 56th Fighter Group, which shot down more German planes than any other American fighter group. Zemke was born in the United States, but his parents were from Germany. Zemke spoke fluent German and some Russian. He was an excellent officer, according to Bob.

The war in Europe officially ended at 23:01 hours central European time on May 8, 1945.

Camp Lucky Strike

Beginning on May 13th, 1945, American B-17s from the 91st Bombardment Group started arriving to evacuate POWs from Stalag Luft I, with a B-17 carrying 30 to 35 POWs on each trip. In three days of continuous landing, loading, and taking off, all the POWs were evacuated.

Along with other former prisoners, Bob was evacuated to Camp Lucky Strike in St. Valery, France, some 45 miles from the northern port city of Le Havre. Demobilization of POWs in Western Europe was conducted primarily through Camp Lucky Strike and nine other camps, eight in France and one in Belgium. These holding areas took their code names from brands of popular cigarettes, hence they became known as the "cigarette camps."

Camp Lucky Strike was the largest cigarette camp, a bustling tent city of 58,000 impatient American troops awaiting transportation back to the United States after victory in Europe. Camp Lucky Strike has been described as both seventh heaven and complete chaos. Former POWs were now designated as Recovered American Military Personnel, or RAMPs. In wartime, as POWs were freed, the War Department ruled that Americans held prisoner for more than 60 days would be returned to the United States rather than returned to their units. This became a bigger challenge when the war ended, and 93,000 RAMPs began to assemble.

Many of the former POWs were wearing the same torn rags they had lived in for months. On the first day there, the RAMPs finally removed their clothing, and their clothes were burned. After immediately taking a shower, they were sprayed with delousing and sanitizer solution. Finally, they were free of lice, fleas, bed bugs, and mites, the constant irritants in the POW camps. Next, new uniforms were issued. This alone gave the former POWs peace of mind and restored a little bit of their humanity.

Upon arrival at Camp Lucky Strike, the RAMPs were given medical examinations, including x-rays, blood and urine tests, and inoculations. Many RAMPs required hospitalization due to respiratory infections or malnourishment. A 350-bed hospital run by the 77th Field Hospital expanded to a 1,500-bed capacity augmented by the 306th General Hospital.

After medical examinations, RAMPs were subjected to a range of forms and applications, as well as debriefings. The intelligence gathered at Lucky Strike also contained information about crew members still missing in action. Some of these reports were used to locate remains or used in court martial or war crimes proceedings. It was emotionally troubling for some to have to record crimes they witnessed or speak about traumatic experiences they had suffered while captive.

The servicemen also finally had decent meals twice a day, although they had to wait in line for long periods in the mess tents. The mess tents were staffed by German POWs overseen by U.S. Army teams advised by medical staff. Many former POWs found ways to supplement their new dietary regimens. In addition to the regular chow lines at Lucky Strike, the Red Cross was there serving donuts.

During Bob's time at Camp Lucky Strike, General Dwight Eisenhower flew in to visit the troops. "He landed there on the airstrip and was surrounded by soldiers, of course," Bob noted. "He liked to mingle with the soldiers. The general asked what he could do for us, and one fellow told him, 'Feed us.' If you don't think a general has power, the next day everything came in there. They sent kitchens and people to work them. We had three meals after that, with little waiting."

Most of the men who had been imprisoned in Germany had lost a significant amount of weight due to the lack of food. Many were emaciated. At six feet tall, Bob had weighed a skinny 154 pounds when he was shot down. Upon arrival at Camp Lucky Strike, he weighed 120 pounds. Many RAMPs had a challenging time adjusting to regular meals. Food regulation at Camp Lucky Strike was the beginning of a long road back to normal digestion and nutrition that would take years. Some of the men who had been eating unregulated for the weeks in between liberation and Lucky Strike were once again placed on restricted diets. Talks on reconditioning the digestive system were delivered and educational posters hung in the mess halls.

The airstrip at Camp Lucky Strike served as the main thoroughfare in the camp, with tent cities arranged in areas designated alphabetically A-D. Each region had its own infrastructure with churches, PX-shops (military retail store), souvenir depots ("booty tents" where one registered their war trophies), barbers, and auditoriums. RAMPs spent time lounging around Lucky Strike, drinking coffee at the American Red Cross Java Junction or reuniting with old friends and crew members from whom they had been separated. RAMPs were accustomed to waiting and some entertainment was provided with movies shown nightly in larger tents. Many slipped through the gate and escaped the camp, as they had desired to do while prisoners. The prime destination for these unsanctioned leaves (as well as sanctioned ones) was Paris, about 100 miles from Lucky Strike. American military hitchhikers were plentiful on the stretch of road from Camp Lucky Strike to the City of Lights.

Paris was not Bob's preferred destination. After three weeks of rehabilitation at Camp Lucky Strike, he was released to go home. Bob, along with 50 others, loaded onto the Liberty ship *SS Samuel Ashe*. The men were housed in the hold of the ship, where it was crowded, dark, and miserable. When Bob and the other last five men prepared to load, the hold was at capacity so the six were housed in the recently vacated gunners' quarters above deck. As part of the ship's crew's quarters, these rooms had real beds. Plus, the six lucky men ate with the officers and crew and stayed above deck with freedom to wander the ship. Liberty ships were not designed for smooth sailing. It was a rough crossing, and Bob was very thankful not to be quartered in the hold of the ship.

It took thirteen days to reach the United States. Bob arrived stateside in Newport News, Virginia, on June 18, 1945, after almost three weeks at Camp Lucky Strike and thirteen days at sea. He had served just under eleven months in combat and as a POW, and he had beaten the odds. Records indicate that 51 percent of Allied aircrews in Europe were killed. Of that number, twelve percent were killed in noncombat situations. In addition, thirteen percent of the airmen who were shot down became POWs. Bob was one of the lucky bomber crew survivors. He successfully completed 32 bombing missions, parachuted out of a doomed B-17 bomber, and survived as a POW in Germany for eight months.

In 1995, on the 50th anniversary of the end of WWII, in a large community celebration at the New Albany High School football field, Bob was awarded the Distinguished Prisoner of War Medal.

Chapter Fourteen

Back Home Again in Indiana

All ten of Bob's fellow crew members survived the war, they all came home.

Bob and Frances on the morning of their wedding.

"I was lucky to get back home," Bob said. "I sure was happy about that. Once I got back to New Albany, I went to the house, and nobody was home. So, the next-door neighbor invited me over, and we sat there in the kitchen, and he asked if I wanted a drink. I took him up on that. The soldiers from World War II were shown a lot of respect. I think it had to do with the fact that we were the ones attacked at Pearl Harbor."

Bob and Frances immediately started planning their wedding. Frances knew that a big wedding was not a good idea. Bob was not ready for crowds of people, and she did not want people coming to gawk at a former POW and flying hero. The wedding was a small, private affair at St. Marks Evangelical and Reformed church in downtown New Albany. They were married on a Wednesday night, July 18, 1945.

New Albany Tribune:
Social Activities by Maxine Hook, July 19, 1945, p. 3:

The wedding of Miss Frances Brown, daughter of Mr. and Mrs. Chester Brown, 1718 E. Spring and T/Sgt. Robert T. Oakes, son of Mr. and Mrs. Robert Oakes, Shelby Street, was solemnized Wednesday night at 8 o'clock in St. Marks Church in the presence of the immediate family and a few friends. The Rev. T. N. Tiemeyer officiated with the single ring ceremony. Wedding music softly played by Mrs. B. C. Holmes, organist, during the ceremony. Miss Marilyn Baxter (Maid of Honor) and Captain Marvin V. Oakes (Best Man), brother of the groom, were the attendants. The bride was dressed in white crepe with white accessories and a white orchid. Miss Baxter wore blue with white accessories and an orchid.

Bob and Frances at their wedding reception at New Albany Country Club. July 19th,1945.

Following the ceremony, a reception was given at the New Albany Country Club.

The couple left on a short trip and upon their return will reside with the bride's parents until August 20, when they will go to Miami, where Sgt. Oakes will be re-assigned.

The bride is a graduate of New Albany High School and attended Indiana University. She is a member of Kappa Alpha Theta sorority.

Sgt. Oakes returned in June after being a prisoner of war in Germany for eight months. He had been overseas since July 1944 and was a member of the 15th Air Force. He also graduated from New Albany High School and attended Purdue University.

Still an enlisted man

Frances' mom would call it an "alley wedding." But as humble and small as the wedding was, Bob and Frances' love knew no bounds. For close to five years, they had been in love. Through separation and war, their love had endured and grown. Finally, they were together. Bob had $500 back pay from the time he spent as a POW. The newlyweds went on a honeymoon to Miami, where they spent a week of joyous fun, dancing, going out to night clubs, enjoying the company of other military couples, and just being together.

The Oakes family reunited after the war. Left to right:Marvin, Bob, Wilma, Katy, and Robert Oakes.

After arriving back in America, Bob was still an enlisted man, and he was assigned to Stout Army Airfield in Indianapolis, where he flew in C-47 planes from San Francisco to Long Island, New York, ferrying former American POWs who had been prisoners of the Japanese. They crisscrossed the country dropping off the ex-POWs at the U.S. Army hospital nearest to their homes. The C-47s were equipped with bunks on one side of the fuselage and seats on the other side. Medical personnel flew along to care for the soldiers. When they arrived in Long Island, having delivered all their POW patients, the air crew would always come up with something wrong with the plane that had to be checked out. This gave them time to go into Manhattan to see the sights.

Bob was deeply affected by the Japanese POWs. He had been a POW, too. As badly as Bob had been treated, he felt that the experiences of the men held captive in the Pacific Theater were even more horrific.

It should be noted that the U.S. Army Air Force lost more crew members in the European Theater (36,461 in combat) than all the Army and Navy airmen lost in the Pacific. A large percentage of crew losses over Europe occurred when Germany held air superiority. The assignment of fighter planes to escort the bombers all the way to their targets, and the development of the P-51 fighters improved the odds. Also, the B-17 airplane went through an evolution of improved engineering and construction modifications throughout the war. By the time Bob was in his Flying Fortress, the B-17 had evolved to the G model. It was a much-improved version over the E and F models. However, flying over enemy territory remained perilous until the very end of the European conflict.

Bob was officially discharged from the Army on October 29, 1945. He was 23 years old. Someone once asked him if he would have enlisted knowing what he was going to experience. "Probably not," he said. "The experience I had was the best of times and the worst of times. I really enjoyed training and flying—that is, until they started shooting back, then it got a little touchy. We all got religion in a hurry. Many of the B-17 crews never made it back. You'd have a tent next to you with ten guys in it, and the next day they're gone. We lost a lot of good men over there."

Settling into civilian life

After the war, there was a severe housing shortage created by so many servicemen returning to civilian life. Bob and Frances first lived for two years with her parents. Their first child, Randy, was born during this time. Before enlisting in the war, Bob had worked as a surveyor at Bowman Field in Louisville for James Hawkins, a family friend. After the war, Bob found himself with a limited skill set. He had dropped out of college, was virtually penniless, and was recently married. Fortunately, Hawkins asked Bob if he wanted to come to his architectural firm, Hawkins & Walker, to see if he liked drafting.

Bob being honored on Veterans Day at St Marks United Church of Christ in New Albany, 2016.

It turned out that Bob did enjoy it, and he was good at it. Bob's income as an entry-level draftsman was low, so all he and Frances could afford was a tiny four-room house in New Albany. Soon, they had their second child, a daughter, Lynne. Eight years later, their third child, Doug, came along. During this time, Bob taught himself the skills he needed to become an architect. With the postwar building boom taking off, it was a good time to be an architect.

After working as a draftsman for ten years, Bob took advantage of the GI Bill, which stipulated that if you worked the required extent of time in that field, you qualified for taking the board exam to become a certified architect. Not only did Bob pass the exam, but he was also the only one of his associates to pass the exam on the first try.

Now working as an architect in a successful firm, the family income steadily increased. The Oakes family was comfortable. They moved to another home, then another, and although it was possible to live in a glamorous house, they chose to keep things simple. Their lifestyle reflected the couple's stable and even-keeled temperaments. Bob could have cared less about what people thought of him. He wasn't out to impress anyone. He always said, "If you have a dime more than you need, you're a rich person."

After working at Hawkins & Walker in the late 40s and early 50s, Bob eventually became a partner in the architectural firm of Walker, Applegate, Oakes, and Ritz. His forte was designing all things mechanical. The list of buildings and sites attributed to the firm is lengthy and includes scores of hospitals, banks, schools, and churches in the region, expanding ever larger as the firm's name and reputation grew. The office was a haven for entertainment as well, with parties throughout the year that included company employees, their families, and clients. He retired once, but he missed being an architect and quickly returned to work. Bob worked as an architect until he was 82.

Bob's easygoing nature was welcomed by all and made befriending him effortless. As laid back as he was, his energy level seemed boundless. He would often come home from work and then go directly across the street to shoot basketball with the neighborhood kids. He also continued to hunt. Then, he discovered golf, and the Oakes family became a golfing family.

Bob golfing at age 93.

He was a member of the Valley View Golf Club and a president of the New Albany Country Club. An avid golfer to the end, Bob could be found on the links well into his 90s.

Bob and Frances had many friends and were very involved in their hometown of New Albany. He was a president of the Rotary Club of New Albany and was a member of the Exchange Club. He and Frances were active members of their church, now St. Marks United Church of Christ. Bob was the on-site architect when St. Marks built its new sanctuary and Sunday school building in 1957. Bob was inducted into the New Albany High School Hall of Fame in 2015.

Bob never abandoned his love of flying. He and his son-in-law, who was also an avid golfer and a pilot, began flying model airplanes. They taught themselves how to build and fly model airplanes, and they flew and built planes regularly. They eventually bought a real airplane, an Aeronca Champion. It was a basic, fly-by-the-seat-of-your-pants aircraft that had to be started manually by pulling on the propellor. They loved it and flew it everywhere.

Bob traveled back to Foggia, Italy, in 2004 with other members of the 97th Bombardment Group. The airfield was still there, operated by the Italians as a fighter base. Escorted by an Italian commander, he was able to go onto the base for a tour of the facilities and the fighter aircraft. They were even able to locate and tour the same building that housed Bob's 340th Bomber Squadron. The buildings were now deserted, and a tomato patch occupied the land where servicemen once pitched their tents. "Unlike much of the rest of Italy, Foggia is relatively featureless, with flat land and airplanes. It was kind of ugly. So, on that trip back there, we went all the way up to Venice, and I saw how beautiful the country was. During the war, I had no idea because I only saw the rest of Italy at 15,000 feet," Bob recalled.

Bob and Frances loved to travel, experiencing as much of life as possible. Perhaps it was facing and overcoming the challenges of poverty as a boy, the trauma of war, the deprivations of POW survival, and the peering into an uncertain future in postwar America as an unemployed newlywed that created his zest for life.

They lived simply, enjoying every minute of their lives together. Bob and Frances were happily married for 67 years.

Frances died December 11, 2012. She was 87 years old. Bob passed away November 10, 2019, the day before Veteran's Day. He was 97 years old.

From left to right, Chet Brown and wife, Jeane Brown, Frances and Bob Oakes. Post war reunion, 1945.

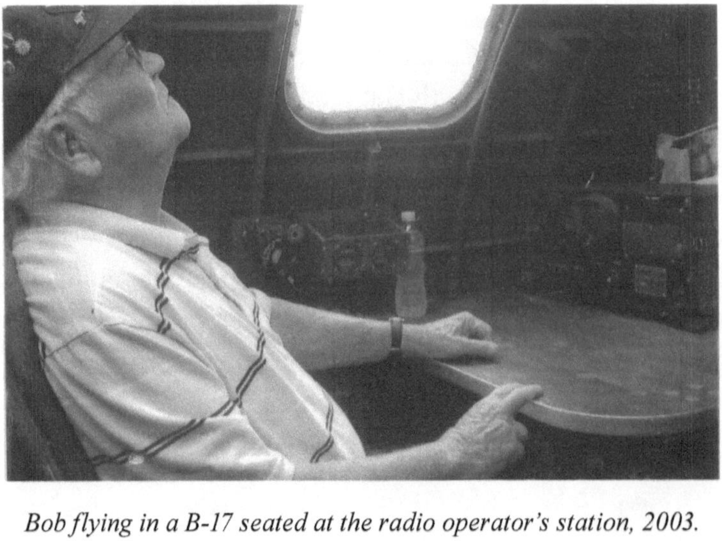

Bob flying in a B-17 seated at the radio operator's station, 2003.

Oakes family on Bob's 90th birthday.
Left to right Bob, Randy, Doug, Lynne, and Frances

Final Thoughts

I was ten years old when I first heard my father talk about his part in WWII. We were at a Girl Scout retreat some five miles out of town on a Friday night. We were 20 yards away from a meeting hall, in an oak grove next to a campfire. There were four of us that night: Dad, Earl, Carl and me. The men were there because their wives and daughters, good Girl Scouts all, were attending a Girl Scout sleepover. We were the guard force keeping them safe from intruders.

I think Carl was the oldest, maybe forty years old. My dad and Earl were thirty-five, and me, a mere ten years old. The first twenty minutes of talk at the campfire was mainly about local sports and their golf games. Carl was the seven-time club champion at our golf club. Dad and Earl were just golf wannabes, listening to Carl's tales of local golf lore.

Then, Carl asked Dad what it was like to be in a B-17 in combat. Dad had been a radio operator in a Flying Fortress. Carl had been a tank commander in a Sherman tank. Earl was a squad leader in the infantry. Dad told a tale of being cold and worried about flak and German fighter planes shooting them out of the sky. He told how his crew often flew in backup planes, because their plane was being repaired. The food was good, and your bed always dry, but the fear of being shot down and killed was always there.

Carl asked Dad about his time as a prisoner of war. Dad was shot down over Czechoslovakia after 32 missions and, near the end of the war, spent eight months in several camps in Poland and Germany.

Dad told his story of parachuting out of the plane with a defective parachute. He talked about how he hurt his ankle when he landed. He recalled having little or no food to eat in the POW camps, and then how he was liberated by the Russians. I had never heard any of this from my father. Stories of his time in the war came from my mother, my dad's parents, and his brother. This was all new to me. It was the first time I had heard it from his mouth.

Carl, after hearing Dad's story, was amazed. He said he always thought being in the Air Force was about the safest place you could be in the war. Carl had commanded a Sherman tank, and he said being in a metal track machine was no piece of cake. During firefights, he wished he was anywhere but where he was. He was confined in a metal container, hot, breathing foul air, deafened by the firing of the tank's 75-mm cannon, and sweating like a pig. He was constantly scared to death that an 88-mm round from a German Tiger tank would slam into them and kill him and his crew of five.

Earl didn't say much other than that he was in Patton's army on their march through France, before and after the Battle of the Bulge. It was near the end of this campaign that Earl's left foot was injured leaving him with a permanent limp. He implied being in the infantry was a series of long marches. It was cold, wet, and very dangerous.

What I took away from that night by the fire was that my father and these men were very young when they went to war. They had no idea what they were getting into, but they went because they felt a need to serve their country. All three were left with permanent scars, both visible and invisible. They were grateful they had survived, and they were always thinking of their comrades who were left behind.

Randy Oakes

(eldest son of Robert and Frances Oakes)

Bibliography

American World War Two Ration Book 3. Photograph. Istock.

https://www.istockphoto.com/account/download/individual/credits? (accessed June28, 2023).

"1937 Flood." Photograph. New Albany, IN: Floyd County Library. https://floydlibrary.catalogaccess.com/photos/15007 (accessed July 20, 2023).

"T/Sgt. Robert J. Hanson of Walla Wall, Washington, Radio Operator On The Boeing B-17 "The Memphis Belle" Is Shown At His Position On The Plane After The 25Th Mission. England 26 May 1943. (U.S. Air Force Number 79235AC)" National Archives. https://catalog.archives.gov/id/204844475 (accessed July 20, 2023).

"I Want You For The U.S. Army Enlist Now"

NAID: 513533Local ID: 44-PA-71Photographs and other Graphic Materials

Covers: 1941–1945

Dates, The creator compiled or maintained the parent series, World War II Posters, between 1942–1945. This item documents the time period of 1941–1945.

https://catalog.archives.gov/id/513533 (accessed July 20,2023).

"Do The Job He Left Behind"

NAID: 513683Local ID: 44-PA-241Photographs and other Graphic MaterialsCovers: 1941–1945

Dates, The creator compiled or maintained the parent series, World War II Posters, between 1942–1945.

This item documents the time period of 1941–1945.

https://catalog.archives.gov/id/513683 (accessed July 20,2023).

Alexander, Bevin. *How Hitler Could Have Won World War II, The Fatal Errors That Led to Nazi Defeat.* New York: Three Rivers Press, 2000.

Ambrose, Stephen E. *Band of Brothers.* New York, New York: Simon and Shuster, 2004.

Ambrose, Stephen E. *D-Day.* New York, New York: Simon and Shuster, 1994, 2014.

Ambrose, Stephen E. *The Victors. Eisenhower and His Boys: The Men of World War II.* New York, New York: Simon and Shuster, 1998.

Armstrong, Roger W. *USA the Hard Way. An Autobiography of a B-17 Crew Member.* Orange County, California: Quail House Publishing Co., 1991.

Atkinson, Rick. *An Army at Dawn.* New York, New York: Simon and Shuster, 2002.

Atkinson, Rick. *The Day of Battle.* New York, New York: Simon and Shuster, 2007.

Atkinson, Richard. *The Guns at Last Light.* New York, New York: Henry Holt and Company, 2013.

Ayres, Travis L. *Bomber Boys, Heroes Who Flew the B-17s in WWII.* New York, New York: NAL Caliber, 2009.

Bowman, Martin. *B-17 Combat Missions. Fighters, Flak, and Forts. First Hand Accounts of Mighty 8th Operations over Germany.* New York, New York: Barnes & Noble, 2007.

Caver, Joseph, Jerome Ennels, and Daniel Haulman. *The Tuskegee Airmen. An Illustrated History: With a Comprehensive Chronology of Missions and Events.* Montgomery, Alabama. New South Books, 2011.

Crane, Conrad C. *American Airpower Strategy in World War II. Bombs, Cities, and Oil.* Lawrence, Kansas: University Press of Kansas, 2016.

Ethell, Jeffrey. *Bombers of WWII.* Ann Arbor, Michigan: Lowe & B. Hould Publishers, 1994.

Gladwell, Malcolm. *The Bomber Mafia.* New York, New York: Hachett Book Group, 2021.

Gulley, Thomas F. (Chairman), Edmond Hicks, Ph. D., William McClintock, Lt. Col. (Ret), Jerry Blackmer, D. D. S., Christopher J. Karas, Lt. Col. (Ret). *The Hour Has Come: The 97th Bomb Group in World War II.* Dallas, Texas: Taylor Publishing Company, 1993.

Hansen, Randall. *Fire and Fury. The Allied Bombing of Germany, 1942-1943.* New York, New York: Penguin Group, 2008.

Hastings, Max. *Bomber Command.* Minneapolis, MN: Zenith Press, 2013.

Hutchinson, James Lee. *The Boys in the B-17, 8th Air force Combat Stories of WWII.* Bloomington, IN: Authorhouse, 2011.

Jablonski, Edward. *Flying Fortress. The Illustrated Biography of the B-17s and the Men Who Flew Them.* Garden City, New York: Doubleday & Company, Inc, 1965.

Janis, Charles G. *Barbed Boredom. A Souvenir Book of Stalag Luft IV.* September 1950.

Kayan, Neil and Stephen G. Hyslop. *Eyewitness to WWII, Unforgettable Stories and Photographs from History's Greatest Conflict.* Washington D. C.: National Geographic Partners, 2012.

Klingaman, William K. *The Darkest Year. The American Homefront 1941-1942.* New York: St. Martin's Press, 2019.

McDowell, Ernest R. *Flying Fortress. The Boeing B-17.* Carrolton, Texas: Squadron/Signal Publications, Inc. 1987.

Merva, George. *Shoo Shoo Baby. A Lucky Lady of the Sky.* Dayton, Ohio: Patterson Productions, 1988.

Miller, Donald L. *Masters of the Air. America's Bomber Boys Who Fought the Air War Against Nazi Germany.* New York: Simon & Shuster, 2006.

Mrazek, Robert J. *To Kingdom Come. An Epic Saga of Survival in the Air War Over Germany.* London, England: NAL Caliber, 2009.

O'Leary, Michael. *Boeing B-17 Flying Fortress. Production Line to Frontline.* Oxford, England: Osprey Publishing, 1998.

Ryan, Cornelius. *The Longest Day.* New York, New York: Simon and Shuster, 1959, 2014.

Shaw, Anthony. *World War II Day by Day.* New York, New York: Chartwell Books, Inc., 2010.

Snyder, Steve. *Shot Down. The True Story of Pilot Howard Snyder and the Crew of the B-17 Susan Ruth.* Seal Beach, California: Seal Beach Publishing, 2015.

Speer, Albert. *Inside the Third Reich.* New York, New York: Avon Books, 1971.

Stout, Jay A. *The Men Who Killed the Luftwaffe. The U.S. Army Air Forces against Germany in World War II.* Mechanicsburg, Pennsylvania: Stackpole Books, 2010.

Tobin, James. *Ernie Pyle's War. America's Eyewitness to World War II.* New York, New York: Free Press, 1997.

Wilmott, H.P. *B-17 Flying Fortress*. Troy, Michigan: Bison Books. 1980.

Yenne, Bill. *Big Week. Six Days That Changed the Course of World War II.* New York, New York: Berkley Caliber, 2012.

'Black Week' : The Darkest Days for the US Army Air Forces, https://www.nationalww2museum.org

Magazines

Special Newsweek Edition, V-E Day, Celebrating 70 Years of Victory, From the Archives, An Oral History of Hitler's Rise and Fall. 2015.

Movies

Twelve O'Clock High, (1949), King, Henry: Zanuk, David F. Producer.

Memphis Belle, (1990), Caton-Jones, Michael: Enigma Production.

Victory by Air. A History of the Aerial Assault Vehicle. Pacific Media. Alicante, Spain: 2009.

World War II. The War in Europe. History Channel. 1983.

Interviews

Janet Applegate interviewed by author December, 14, 2021

Betty Barksdale interviewed by author July 10, 2022

End Notes

45 As war correspondent Ernie Pyle observed, "you realized vividly how everybody in America," *Ernie Pyle's War,* 105.

46 Before the Pearl Harbor attack, *The Darkest Year,* 76.

46 If the Japanese could bomb, *The Darkest Year*, 76.

46 Familiar faces were missing throughout the nation, (*Indiana Servicemen Index*)

46 Paul McNutt, head of the War, *The Darkest Year*, 198.

47 Even something as routine as weather, *The Darkest Year*, 86.

47 At the same time German submarines, *The Darkest Year*, 91.

47 By February 1941 the Navy admitted, *The Darkest Year*. 132.

47 By April the number of American, *The Darkest Year*, 206.

49 For example, the army received 50 to 70 of, *The Darkest Year,* 137

64 "A few years ago, I discussed my cadet experience," *USA the Hard Way*, 10.

83 In WWII, from 1939 until February 1944, Germany was decidedly in, *Big Week*, xiv.

83 The world witnessed the integral part, *The Flying Fortress,* 286.

84 "Never in the field of,"

https://en.wikipedia.org>wiki>Never_was_so_much_owed_...

84 Some believe this was Hitler's, *How Hitler Could Have Won WWII*, 63.

85 This was a trial-and-error process, *Fire and Fury,* 131.

85 "Of all the combat jobs in the American services," *Bombers of WII*, 7.

85 It was at Casablanca that the decision, *The Flying Fortress,* 113-114.

85 This would include bombing German submarine construction, *Flying Fortress*. 114.

85 Early on the Allies knew that, *The Men Who Killed the Luftwaffe,* 155.

86 "It was one of the great air battles," Flying Fortress, 130-131.

86 60 bombers and 600 crewmen, *The Men Who Killed the Luftwaffe,* 145.

86 Along with the crippling of the German airplane industry, *The Victors*, 59.

86 In *The Victors* Stephen Ambrose writes, "The bombers went to work, dropping", *The Victors*, 59.

87 Don Miller wrote in *Masters of the Air* that "Seventy-seven percent, *Masters of the Air*, 7.

87 The German economy was more resilient, *Big Week*, 240.

87 It took time and fuel to train air crews, *Big Week*, 244.

88 Still, the accuracy of the Fifteenth Air force bombing had risen to, *Big Week*, 244.

89 At first, heavy bombers were also used to attack, *Masters of the Air*, 148.

89 The P-51 was a superb fighter plane, *The Men Who Killed the Luftwaffe,* 160

89 It was equipped with six .50 caliber weapons, *The Men Who Killed the Luftwaffe,* 160

90 "The total number of (Tuskegee) escorted," *The Tuskegee Airmen, 103.*

90 "On the longest fighter-escort mission," *The Tuskegee Airmen*, 103.

92 When Bob began flying missions in 1944, *Masters of the Air*, 318.

109 "The B-17, I think, was the best combat plane," *Flying Fortress*, xiv.

110 "The B-17 was as tough an airplane", *Flying Fortress*, xiv.

110 "By far the best bomber we", *Flying Fortress*, xiv.

110 The B-17 became the most celebrated, *Flying Fortress*, 37.

110 Of the 1.5 million tons of bomb dropped, *Boeing B-17 Flying Fortress*, 97.

110 The Army Airforce produced a, *Big Week*, 80.

110 Before December 1943, only 30 percent of, *The Boys in the B-17,* 37.

110 A total of 12,731 B-17's were, *Flying Fortress,* 309.

110 The bomber command leaders were, *The Boys in the B-17,* 45.

111 The Germans were not impressed, *Flying Fortress*, 260.

111 Even as late as August 1943, the German, *Flying Fortress*, 260.

111 Hitler was also delusional about the, *Fire and Fury,* 135.

111 Even so, the Luftwaffe continued to inflict terrible losses, *The Men Who Killed the Luftwaffe,* 129.

111 It was designed to be a long-range, *Flying Fortress*, 312.

111 Thousands of modifications were made *Flying Fortress*, 312.

112 Each B-17 cost $270,000 to produce. *The Men Who Killed the Luftwaffe,* 164.

112 As Jay Stuart wrote in *The Men Who Killed the Luftwaffe,* 171.

112 It was easy to fly, stable, *B-17 Flying Fortress*, 32.

112 Many B-17's endured seemingly, *Flying Fortress*, xiii.

112 No wonder their crews held the, *Flying Fortress*, xiii.

113 "The miracle was that the Air Force," *Flying Fortress*. 142.

114 The average age of a B-17 crew member, *The Boys in the B-17,* 2.

115 Only 15% of the United States, *The Men Who Killed the Luftwaffe*, 277.

115 "To put 500 bombers in the," *B-17 Flying Fortress*, 51.

116 Done to precision, it was lethal, *The Men Who Killed the Luftwaffe*, 99.

116 It could direct bombs to hit, *The Big Week*, 37.

116 "This precision compensated for," *Flying Fortress*, 322.

117 Bombardier's Oath, http://www.merkki.com/bombardiers of usaaf in world wa.htm

117 "Navigators would pick up their charts," *B-17 Combat Missions*, 44.

118 Written in The Pilot's Training Manual, *Flying Fortress*, 324.

118 Over 150 instruments were, *Master of the Air,* 84.

119 "Bomber pilots suffered much," *Masters of the Air*, 285.

119 The best way to knock out a B-17, *B-17 Combat Missions*, 30.

119 The engineer was in charge of, *Flying Fortress*, 315.

120 He assisted the pilots with monitoring, *Flying Fortress*, 327.

120 "Bomb bay racks were fitted to carry," *Flying Fortress*. 315.

121 The Command Radio provided, *B-17 Combat Missions*, 57.

122 The ball turret was a 43-inch, *B-17 Combat Missions*, 113.

122 "The ball turret could be moved," *Flying Fortress*, 54.

122 Then the hatch above him, *B-17 Combat Missions,* 113.

123 "But regardless of the fact that," *The Men Who Killed the Luftwaffe*, 140.

124 He kept the pilots informed of what, *B-17 Combat Missions*, 127.

124 "the tail gunner hunched," *Masters of the Air*, 82.

124 Of all the positions, the tail gunner, *Masters of the Air*, 93.

124 "The equipment of survival both," *Masters of the Air*, 89.

131 "The Eighth and Fifteenth joined," *Fire and Fury*, 205.

131 In these raids, the British bombers, *Masters of the Air*, 321

139 This same exposure and fear, *Masters of the Air*, 476.

143 When Bob was flying combat missions over, *Masters of the Air*, 318.

144 When on the ground, the crew members were described as, *Masters of the Air*, 318.

144 You parachuted out of a doomed, *Masters of the Air*, 14.

144 War correspondent Ernie Pyle described, *Ernie Pyle's War,* 199.

145 "...the greater courage was exercised," *The Men Who Killed the Luftwaffe*, 366.

146 Pilots, navigators, and bombardiers, *B-17 Combat Missions*, 57

147 Bombers often had 200 to 300 flak holes, *Masters of the Air*, 317.

148 Strategic Bombing, as defined by the Air Force, *Masters of the Air*, 31.

148 By using forced laborers from territories, *USA The Hard Way*, 135.

152 crews completed eleven missions before, "*'Black Week'*: The Darkest Days for the US Army Air Forces," https:// www. nationalww2 museum.org.

154 "The parachutes themselves were," *Master of the Air*, 85.

156 This order encouraged German civilians, *Flying Fortress*, 154.

159 Ninety-eight men from New Albany were killed in action. *New Albany Tribune*, 10/8/1963, Sec 5. P.12.

163 "Our airmen who were prisoners of the Germans," *Masters of the Air*, 487.

164 They questioned Bob about nationality, *Barbed Boredom*, 10

165 "I believe, that of all the Prisoners of War phases," *Barbed Boredom*, 9

166 Opened in the summer of 1944, Stalag Luft IV was, *USA The Hard Way*, 155

167 "The big event was when the," *USA The Hard Way*, 159

172 A few clergymen were allowed in POW camps, *Barbed Boredpm*, 36

172 "these men who were alive but not living." *Barbed Boredom*

174 Originally opened in 1941 as a British POW camp, *USA The Hard Way*, 211

177 Along with their many uncertainties, the prisoners, *Masters of the Air, 493, 499, 500*

177 Each POW received five Red Cross packages, *USA The Hard Way*, 238

178 Colonel Hubert Zemke, the Senior Allied Officer, *USA The Hard Way*, 212

178 Zemke was the former commander of the 56th Fighter Group, *Masters of the Air*, 282

178 Beginning on May 13th, 1945, American B-17s, *USA The Hard Way*, 279

182 Records indicate that 51 percent of Allied aircrews in Europe, *Masters of the Air*, 471

219 Specifications of B-17G, *Flying Fortress*, 310-311

Glossary

Air Medal

Awarded for every six missions flown by a bomber crewman.

Allies

The alliance of the United Kingdom, Soviet Union, and the United States. Other countries were China, Canada, Australia, New Zealand, South Africa, Brazil, Mongolia, Mexico, Poland, Czechoslovakia, Norway, Netherlands, Belgium, Luxembourg, Free France, Ethiopia, Greece, Yugoslavia, Philippines.

WWII Army Ranks (private through major sergeant)

Private, Private First Class, Corporal, Sergeant, Staff Sergeant, Technical Sergeant, 1st Sergeant, Major Sergeant

Army Air Corps

The aerial part of the U.S. Army from 1926-1941

Army Air Force

The aerial part of the U.S. Army from 1941-1947.

Axis Alliance

The alliance of Nazi Germany, the Kingdom of Italy, and the Empire of Japan. Minor countries in this alliance were the Kingdom of Hungary,

Kingdom of Romania, Kingdom of Bulgaria, Republic of Finland, Slovak Republic, State of Croatia, and the Kingdom of Thailand. The Alliance was established in 1936 and lasted until their defeat in 1945 in World War II.

Alps Mountain Range

The Alps are the highest and largest mountain range completely in Europe. The range stretches across the countries of Monaco, France, Switzerland, Italy, Liechtenstein, Germany, Austria, and Slovenia. The highest elevation is 15,776 feet.

B-17 Flying Fortress

Heavy duty bomber with four engines used in WWII. Flown with a ten-person crew flying in sub-zero temperatures and requiring oxygen masks while flying at an altitude of 25,000 feet or higher.

Bail Out

To parachute out of an airplane that is no longer able to fly.

Ball bearings

Small metal balls that facilitate moving parts in machinery.

Ball turret

A small spherical-shaped gun position that was attached to the bottom of a B-17 bomber airplane. The turret was manned by one person who operated two machine guns. It rotated to enlarge the shooting area the gunner could utilize.

Battery

A tactical unit of artillery, usually composed of six guns and the men to fire them.

Battle of Britain

A series of aerial combats during World War II that took place between British and German aircraft during the autumn of 1940 and that included the severe bombardment of British cities. The British victory in this air battle discouraged Hitler from attacking England.

BBC (British Broadcasting Corporation)

A British organization that broadcasts on television, radio, and the internet. It provided reliable news, entertainment, and hope during WWII.

Blitzkrieg (Lightening War)

An intense military campaign intended to bring about a swift victory. Infantry, armor, and airpower combined with speed and power to conquer an enemy's forces.

Bombardment Group or Bomb Group

A unit of organizational command and control group of the United States Army Air Forces (USAAF) during WW II.

Cadet School

A pilot training program that trains pilots, navigators, and bombardiers. Candidates were required to score high on a qualifying exam and meet physical requirements to enter their desired program.

Carpet Bombing

A bombing attack that destroys everything in a wide area.

Crew Chief

Head mechanic of a ground crew assigned to keep an airplane in flying shape.

D-Day

The day (June 6, 1944) in WWII on which Allied forces invaded northern France by means of beach landings in Normandy. It was the largest amphibious invasion in military history.

Flak

Flak is a concentration of German Flugabwehrkanone (also referred to as Fliegerabwehrkanone) meaning "aircraft-defense-cannon," the original purpose of the weapon. In English, "flak" became a generic term for ground anti-aircraft fire/guns.

Fighter Escort

Fighter airplanes were used to fly along with the bomber airplanes to long range targets. The Allied fighters engaged enemy fighters who were attacking the bombers. The fighters escorted the bombers on their way to and from the bombers' targets deep in enemy territory.

Fuselage

The main body of an airplane.

G.I.

G.I. evolved into a term that refers to a soldier in the United States armed forces, primarily the army. It is a term originally used in WWII. May have originated from the term Government Issue.

Heavy Bombers

Heavy bombers were designed to carry a large load of bombs for a long-distance during WWII. The heavy bombers used in WWII were the B-17 Flying Fortress, the B-24 Liberator, and the B-29 Superfortress.

Luftwaffe

Luftwaffe (German: "air weapon") was a component of the German armed forces tasked with the offensive air war and the air defense of Germany.

Messerschmidt Bf 109

The Messerschmidt Bf 109 is a German World War II fighter aircraft that was the backbone of the Luftwaffe's fighter airplanes.

MIA

MIA is a term used in the military to denote a soldier who is missing in action.

Morse code

A system of dots and dashes (electrical pulses of varied lengths) that represent letters of the alphabet. The Morse code symbols used in this book to designate written correspondence from Bob say "my darling."

Newsreels

A short film of news and current affairs, formally made for showing as part of the program in a movie theater.

PFC Stripes

Private first class is a military rank held by junior enlisted personnel in many armed forces. Stripes are a ranking insignia worn on the sleeve of the uniform.

POW

Prisoner of war.

Purple Heart

The Purple Heart medal is presented to service members who have been wounded or killed as a result of enemy action while serving in the U.S. military.

Signals sheet

A sheet of paper that was given out to pilots, navigators, bombardiers, and radio operators of a bomber crew before a mission. the information on the sheet gave codes and special signals for the day.

Sortie

A sudden rushing out of troops from a defensive position to attack the enemy. Example: an airplane leaving its home base and flying into enemy territory.

Squadron

An operational unit in an air force consisting of two to twelve aircraft and the personnel required to fly them.

Submarine pen

A well protected submarine base. Submarines were housed and repaired in these super large structures that could not be significantly damaged by bomber attacks.

Turret

A gunner's fixed or movable enclosure in an airplane.

Washed out

A person who has failed a course of training or study, or deemed unable to continue that training, is said to have washed out.

Wehrmacht

German armed forces especially of Germany from 1935 to 1945.

Bob's list of foods to eat when he got back home

from his POW notebook

Steaks

T-bone
Sirloin
Round
Aged Beef Smothered with Mushrooms
Porter House
Rib (Prime Beef)
Seven
Shoulder Round

Stack Pies
Corn Fritters
Coconut Cake
Chicken Noodle Soup
Banana Cake
Devil's Food Cake
Deviled Ham
Ginger Snaps

Chopped Wieners with Scrambled Eggs & Onions Scrambled together
To Try-French Frying Sardines
Barbecued Fish
Baked Opossum
Fried Cabbage
Venison-All Kinds
Fried Turtle & Turtle Soup
Aged Cheddar Cheese
Pinto Beans Cooked with Ham Bone
Chitlins
Blind Robbins & Beer

Chow-Chow
Bread & Butter Pickles
Kosher Pickles

Oyster Loaf
Cantaloupes
Watermelon

Half of a Banana Stuffed with Mayonnaise & Mustard Wrapped in Bacon and Baked

Mexican Revolution

Swedish Smorgasbord

Cottage Cheese & Onions

Mushrooms and Chicken Livers Fried

Fried Peas and Bacon

Fried Green Tomatoes Rolled in Crackers

Noodles

Persimmon Pudding

Left Over Waffles Heated with Chocolate

Ritz Crackers Warmed with Peanut Butter

Welsh Rare Bit Graham Crackers Baked with

Abilene Steak Marshmallows

Sauteed Chopped Pork and Onions

Chocolate Waffles

Sauteed Fish Fillets in Garlic & Onions

Liver Pate

Breaded Carrots and Quail

Fried Oatmeal with Syrup

Hot Waffles Covered with Ice Cream, Butterscotch, and Nuts

French Fried Onions

Ham Baked in Ginger Ale

Hot Donuts with Peanut Butter in the Hole and Ice Cream

Fried Shrimp

Hamburger Sandwich with Decorations

Raw Oysters

Fried Bread with Egg in Center

Sardine Salad

Corn Beef Fritters

Crepe Suzette

Fried Scallops

Fried Clams

Clam Cakes

Baked Clams on Half Shell

Pickled Prawns

Smoked Herring

Stuffed Crab

Clam Chowder

Fried Mush

Chow Mein

Egg Fu Young

Veal Sweet Meat with Mushrooms

Fresh Fried Tenderloin

Hot Tamales

Shrimp Cocktail

Brains and Eggs

Chicken in the Rough

Fried Flounder

Fried River Perch

Mushroom Soup

Fritos (in the South)

Pecan Pie

Peanut Butter and Jelly Sandwich

Kraft Cheese Spread

Potato Chips

Tuna Fish and Chicken Salad Sandwiches

Ham Salad Sandwiches

Raisins

Edam Cheese

Bay Bud Gouda Cheese

Spam

Plum Pudding

Chocolate Coated Graham Crackers

Sardine Sandwich

Box of Pure Caramels

Cream Puffs

Jelly Beans

Fried Pies

Swiss Cheese

Milk Chocolate

Peanut Butter Fudge

Hershey Chocolate Mixed with Whipped Cream

Chocolate, Powdered Milk, and Raisins

White Castle Hamburgers

Marshmallow Peanut Butter Cookies

Ice Box Pies

Cold Luncheon Meats with Potato Salad

Home Cooked

Macaroni and Cheese

Steak and Spaghetti

Fried Oysters

Chicken Dumplings

Fried Chicken

Candied Sweet Potatoes

Pancakes

Corn Bread

Fried Potatoes and Onions

Light Bread Biscuits

Vegetable Soup

Hot Milk over Toast

French Fried Bread

Strawberry Shortcake

Toasted Cheese Sandwich with Jelly

Bread Pudding

Fried Liver and Onions

Chili

Spaghetti and Meatballs

Biscuits and Strawberry Preserves

Ham and Eggs

Canadian Bacon

Potato Salad

Baked Beans

Scalloped Potatoes

Creamed Peas & Salmon

Meat Loaf with Bacon and Ketchup

Salmon Croquette

Chipped Beef Gravy on Toast

Mashed Potatoes and Gravy

Chicken Dressing

Fruit Salad

Spanish Rice

String Beans and Corn

Banana Pudding

Brussel Sprouts

Chuck Roast

Fried Liverwurst

Buckwheat Cakes

Fried Apples and Ham

Barbecued Spare Ribs

Sour Kraut and Pork Chops

Sour Kraut and Wieners

Fried Eggplant

Peas and Carrots

Fried Corn

Corn on the Cob

City Chicken

Fried Spam

Poached Eggs on Toast

Spinach

Swiss Steaks

Cauliflower

Baked Potatoes

Asparagus Tips Fried in Onions

Pork Sausage

Cole Slaw

Ham & Cabbage

Beef Stew

Breaded Veal Cutlets

Creamed Chicken on Biscuits

Virginia Baked Ham

Stuffed Peppers

Hot Beef & Hot Pork Sandwiches

Deviled Eggs

Bean Soup

Tomato Soup

Breaded Tomato Soup

Spaghetti with Chopped up Wieners

Apple Sauce

Cranberry Sauce

Rice Pudding

Lamb Fries

Head Cheese

Creamed Celery

Pastries

Huckleberry Pie

Blueberry Pie

Gooseberry Pie

Chocolate Eclairs

Apple Pie with Cheese

Blackberry Cobbler

Chocolate Cake

Cookies and Milk

Home Baked Rolls

Ginger Bread

Brownies

Cherry Pie

Fried Pies

Mince Meat Pie

Raisin Bread Toasted

Rye Bread (Jewish)

Ice Box Cookies

Peanut Butter Cookies

Marshmallow cookies

Angel Food Cake

Fruit Cake

Macaroons

Pineapple Upside Down Cake

Hot Cross Buns

All Bran Muffins

Pumpkin Pie

Chocolate pie

Custard Cream Pie

Sweet Potato Pie

Peach Pie

Raspberry Pie

Danish Pastries

Apple Turnovers

Coffee Cakes

Cinnamon Rolls

Pecan Pie

Nut Bread

Cherry, Apple Dumplings

Parker House Rolls

Chess Pie

B-17G Bomber Specifications

Wing Span. 103’ 9.38”

Fuselage Length. 74’ 8.9”

Four Engines. Wright R-1820-97 1,000 HP

Weight Empty. 36,134 lbs

Weight Gross 38,200 lbs

Top Speed 302 mph

Cruising Speed 160 mph

Maximum Range. 3,750 miles

Service Ceiling. 35,000’

Armament Thirteen .50 caliber machine guns

Crew. Ten men-Pilot, Co Pilot, Bombardier, Navigator, Engineer, Radio Operator, 2 Waist Gunners, Ball Turret Gunner, Tail Gunner

Acknowledgements

My daughter, Jennifer, took this chaos of a writing endeavor and worked her magic to transform it into a real book. Jennifer, a professional marketer and graphic artist, employed her skills of designing, formatting, and rewriting to bring this story about her grandparents to fruition. She provided me with a valuable perspective from her generation, the next generation removed from WWII. There are not enough thanks to express my gratitude for her help.

I have been trying to keep up with my big brother, Randy, my whole life. As an author, he is four books ahead of me, but I'm trying to follow his exemplary literary achievements. His invaluable experience, talent, and encouragement have been constant sources of inspiration and knowledge throughout my life. One could not have a better big brother. Thank you, Randy, for all your help as well as your memories about our mom and dad.

My endless thanks to my Step-Daughter Terri, who is always ready to help and to listen.

Linda, Donna, Kathy, Kris, and Debbie are my dear friends who are always there to listen and encourage me. They have kept my perspective in focus, helped me keep on task, and encouraged me along the rough stretches. They have given their honest criticism, which is the best help a true friend can give.

My cousin Andrea, with whom I spent many hours sewing doll clothes at our Grandma Oakes' house, provided priceless family information and photos. Her knowledge of the family and her infectious sense of humor continue to be a source of inspiration.

Wayne contributed his wealth of aviation knowledge and his belief in my ability to compose this book. He shared a love of flying and golf with my dad.

My son, Remy, helped my dad start his journey of recovery, acceptance, and education about his WWII experiences by asking him to share his story.

I am deeply indebted to The National WWII Museum in New Orleans for the constant inspiration and dedication to preserve the memories of WWII, and for their assistance to me in compiling this book. Every day The National WWII Museum exemplifies its mission as it welcomes thousands of visitors.

A special word of thanks to the Friday, first-shift volunteer crew at The National WWII Museum, who have been a source of encouragement, information, and inspiration.

I am sure my two editors were heaven sent. A special thank you to Carl and Mary Kramer for their expertise, patience, and, most of all, their friendship. Thank goodness that Hawaiian cruise was canceled at the last minute!

A heartfelt thank you to St. Marks UCC Church, which played such a significant role in Bob and Frances' lives, even unto their great grandchildren. Thank you to my St. Marks family for your prayers, stories, and support.

A special thank you to Janet Applegate and Betty Barksdale, both lifelong friends of Bob and Fran, who shared precious memories and information.

Thank you to the staff of The Floyd County Library System, New Albany Central, Indiana Room, who were very helpful with my research on New Albany during WWII.

A big thanks to Tracy for helping me with my first venture into writing.

Without Maggie Oster's help this work would not have been finished. Many thanks for your time and expertise.

My children and grandchildren have been my constant inspiration. This story is for them, so that they will always know the sacrifices and courage of their ancestors.

About the Author

Lynne Oakes is a retired educator and life-long fiber artist. She has a Bachelor of Science degree in Education from Louisiana State University and Masters degrees in Education from Indiana University. Lynne divides her time between New Orleans, Louisiana, and New Albany, Indiana, and works as a professional weaver.

For years, Lynne often accompanied her father, Bob, when he gave talks about his experiences during WWII, plus she lived with him for the final eight years of his life. That gave her innumerable opportunities to hear even more about his experiences. It wasn't until after her father's death that she found her mother's diaries and her father's letters. This inspired her to write about their story and convey the emotions and experiences that Bob and Frances endured during the worst conflict in human history.

www.ingramcontent.com/pod-product-compliance
Lightning Source LLC
LaVergne TN
LVHW041700070526
838199LV00045B/1142
* 9 7 9 8 8 9 4 1 9 1 8 8 1 *